MEMOIRS OF A
Jamaican
MEDIA-MAN

CAREY ROBINSON

Editor: Kenisha T. Duff
Cover Design: Sanya Dockery
Book Design, Layout & Typesetting: Sanya Dockery

Published by LMH Publishing Limited
Suite 10-11
Sagicor Industrial Complex
7 Norman Road
Kingston C.S.O., Jamaica
Tel.: (876) 938-0005; 938-0712
Fax: (876) 759-8752
Email: lmhbookpublishing@cwjamaica.com
Website: www.lmhpublishing.com

Printed in the USA   ISBN: 978-976-8202-88-8

NATIONAL LIBRARY OF JAMAICA CATALOGUING-IN-PUBLICATION DATA
Robinson, Carey
    Memoirs of a Jamaican media-man / Carey Robinson
    p. ; cm.
ISBN 978-976-8202-88-8 (pbk)
1. Robinson, Carey, 1924 -   2. Journalists – Jamaica – Biography
3. Jamaica – Biography   I. Title
920   dc 22

Contents

Foreword

Carey Robinson grew up in British Jamaica, a part of the Empire upon which "the sun never sets". The Empire was presided over by monarchs: uniformed Kings with grave faces and bejewelled Queens dressed in flowing robes.

Jamaica was a complicated mix of the aristocratic British Imperial and parliamentary culture, and the exuberant and jaunty spirit of the United States. The country's conservative high school educational system was based on the civilization of ancient Greece and Rome, and the military and naval adventures of Britain all over the world.

The heroes were men such as Drake, Raleigh, Cook, Rodney, Horatio Nelson, Kitchener, etc. The Empire rested firmly on the English class system and was won by thousands of poor young men led by a privileged officer class, who shed their blood in "glorious" battles. That, combined with American radio programmes and films, enlivened the minds of the privileged Jamaican youths.

No Jamaican history was taught in schools like Calabar, which Robinson attended. There was a profound academic ignorance of the country, its resources and the plight of the poor and the marginalized. Well-to-do Jamaicans were taken by surprise when the workers took to the streets in 1938 demanding better wages and working conditions.

When World War II broke out and the Germans under Adolf Hitler threatened to engulf Europe, Jamaican young men and women hastened to join the Royal Air Force and the Auxiliary

Territorial Service – eager to fight for "King and Country" as an earlier generation had done during World War I.

They left behind a Jamaica which was in ferment, with the workers led by Bustamante and St. William Grant, and the intellectuals driven by the vision of Oxford educated Norman Washington Manley. Trade unions and political parties were being formed and the country was inching towards Universal Adult Suffrage.

The old social presumptions of natural rule by an elite over the mass of people were being challenged and undermined as Jamaica struggled on the road to self-government and independence. It was during this period of social change that the electronic media in Jamaica began to emerge.

Robinson, instead of joining the uniformed stream of his contemporaries participating in the struggle against Nazi Germany, applied to and was accepted by Howard University in the United States. He was immediately confronted with Jim Crow. At the time he felt that all that stood between him and Jim Crow was his British passport and the image of the young Princess Elizabeth. Americans tended not to mess with you if they knew you were a British subject. But Robinson soon fell in with a group of militant West Indian students who wanted independence and a break-away from the old colonial system. Then one day, Norman Manley came to address members of the student body. It was a great talk and was very well received. Robinson felt proud to be a Jamaican. If his country could produce a man like Norman Manley then it could challenge and change the old oppressive system. He soon abandoned his original plans to study medicine and went in for psychology and history. His master's thesis was fortunately about George William Gordon and the 1865 Morant Bay Rebellion. Many years later, Gordon and Paul Bogle were made National Heroes.

Returning home after graduating, Robinson embarked on a quest to find work that would allow him to make a contribution to nation-building.

Growing Up

In 1932, a thirty eight year old wireless engineer named John Francis Grinan built a small, amateur radio station in Jamaica. He called it VP5PZ, and it was operated for brief periods. The few people who had short wave radios had depended on stations in the U.S. and the U.K. for news and entertainment. Television, of course, was nowhere in sight.

The first time I listened to a radio broadcast was when my family went across to a neighbor's house to hear the heavyweight boxing fight between Joe Louis (the Brown Bomber) and Max Baer (the Livermore Butcher). Joe Louis won. That was in September, 1935.

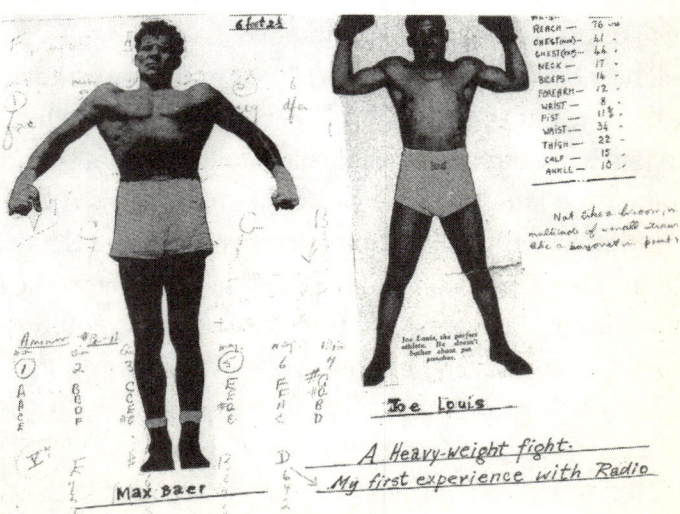

Max Baer vs Joe Louis

We didn't have a radio, but we had a piano, which was a prized possession in those days, and a sort of status symbol. My sister took piano lessons. We had frequent singing sessions, especially when there were visitors.

During this time I was attending a private secondary school. The father of the principal was a Seventh Day Adventist Missionary who taught at the school. He loved to beat and would pounce on me from behind while I was at the blackboard, if my calculations were not correct. The suddenness of his attacks alone were unnerving. I never forgot his savagery.

I was transferred to Calabar High School, which was on Slipe Road at the time. The Headmaster was a Baptist Parson who also loved to beat. Unfortunately, my father told him that he expected him to beat me. The Headmaster would sometimes line up a number of boys and order them to touch their toes. Then he would go from boy to boy, lashing ferociously with his cane. Each boy would pop-up straight with a cry of pain as the cane bit into his posterior. I really believe that the Headmaster thoroughly enjoyed every stroke he delivered. He would repeat the process three or so times before he was finished.

As a new boy at Calabar, I was placed in the lowest form with boys who were either white or of "light" complexion. Whenever I tried to join in their games, their leaders told them not to play with me. Some time later, when I was inevitably absorbed into their ranks, they decided to go to Bournemouth Club one Saturday to swim in the pool. Only people who looked like them were welcome at Bournemouth in those days. So they debated among themselves whether they should ask me to go. They were not wicked boys. That was just the way Jamaica was in those days.

For a very brief period I was the fastest sprinter at school in the under fifteen class. I was chosen to represent Calabar at the annual School Boys Athletic Championships. But I was so distrustful of my abilities and so fearful of losing that I hid beneath the stands until the hundred yards race was over. The race was won by the boy who was put in as my substitute. He later became my brother-in-law.

I remember the three very tall Wint brothers: Arthur, Douglas and Lloyd. They were runners. They berated me for missing the race. Arthur Wint went on to become an internationally famous athlete and was one of the 4 x 440 Relay team (including Herb McKenley, Les Laing and George Rhoden) which won the gold medal for Jamaica in the 1952 Helsinki Olympics. They put Jamaica on the map as a country of serious runners.

Herb McKenley was also at Calabar in my time. Herb ran like a crazy horse. He played one or two matches on the first eleven football (soccer) team, but often ran so fast that he left the ball behind.

In 1938 there was trouble with sugar workers. They wanted more pay and better working conditions. The unrest spread into Kingston where we were living. Workers took over the streets, and my mother sent someone to fetch me from school and take me home.

A man, who called himself Bustamante, suddenly materialized from among the workers on the estates and on to the streets of Kingston. He seemed like a threat because the mass of neglected working people were ready to follow him.

My maternal grandfather, who was then about sixty-seven and had retired, was moved to exclaim:

"Who is this Bustamante?"

He wrote his eldest daughter and said:

"The Hooligan elements are bent on a 'show down... they mean to have a weltering bloodshed...

The Politicians and self-appointed leaders of the people are of no use at all, save to exploit the illiterate masses for their own selfish ends. What is to become of the population of this place...only God knows. I foresee chaos and ruin, and the last state being worst than the first. But perhaps I am a pessimist."

The gaunt Bustamante and the haranguing mobs of workers unsettled my grandfather. But I think what really alarmed him was what happened to Uncle Billy, his youngest child.

Uncle Billy had a peculiar life-style. He was a tall, large, powerful young man, in his twenties. He liked to wear jodhpurs (riding breeches) and he had a big, grey horse. If he lost his temper Uncle Billy was likely to get into a fist fight.

He used to take the horse down to Kingston Waterfront and into the sea for a swim. One day when the streets were full of disgruntled workers, Uncle Billy rode downtown on his horse like a prince. The sight of this apparently privileged young man, wearing jodhpurs and mounted on a spirited horse, angered the workers. They dragged him from the saddle and took away the horse. Later, Uncle Billy managed to recover the horse, but the incident probably offended his macho instinct.

Shortly afterwards, Uncle Billy was in a car driven by his boss, Dr. Ken Evans, who was in charge of the government laboratory. They went along North Street which was full of workers, and then on to Slipe Pen Road which was also full of workers. The doctor tried to turn into the compound of the laboratory through the gate on Slipe Pen Road. The car bounced someone in the crowd. That was a signal for explosion. In those days motor-car people belonged to the privileged group.

Men tore open the door of the car and began dragging out the doctor. He managed to draw his gun and fired a shot in the air. That made matters worse. He was pulled out and beaten. Uncle Billy jumped out of the car and started to fight off the attackers. They struck him with clubs and fists, but with the help from the staff at the lab, he managed to get his boss through the gate, which was then slammed and bolted. But Uncle Bill had received a terrible beating.

My father was then superintendent of medical stores (Island Medical storekeeper) and his office was in the Government Laboratory building. After Dr. Evans was dragged inside, the angry mob attacked and besieged the building. My father had to take refuge beneath his desk from a storm of stones, bricks and

bottles which flew through the windows of his office. He was pinned down there until armed soldiers and policemen arrived and drove off the mob. When it was time to go home, my father took off his tie and jacket (the uniform of the privileged), abandon his hat (which he always wore when going out) and walked through the dangerous streets trying to look innocuous. But for all the work he was called upon to do, and the responsibilities he had, he was a poorly paid man himself.

A day or so later, I went to see Uncle Billy. He was in bed. His back and shoulders were a mass of black and blue. He had to lie on his stomach. I think this incident was really what alarmed my grandfather.

About a year after the disturbance my family got a radio. It was pure joy to crouch before the magic box, through which came exciting things from the outside world. Cowboy series (The Lone Ranger, Tom Mix, etc), Mystery (The Showdown, The Green Hornet, The Inner Sanctum), comedy (Bob Hope, Jack Benny, George Burns and Gracie Allen), and a cheerful morning programme called the Breakfast Club (no relation to the Jamaican talk-show of later days).

World War II broke out in September, 1939. The next year, John Francis Grinan, the wireless engineer, presented his amateur radio station (VP5PZ) to the Government. The gift was probably his contribution to the "the War Effort." The station was given a new name: ZQI. It was on the air for about two hours a day; mostly some news, classical music and little "local stuff."

When I was in the "troublesome" fourth form, I made my first venture into journalism. We had a "Rag" (paper) called "The Daily Red" which I helped to write and illustrate. It contained the foolish jokes and nonsense typical of mid-teen boys.

Movies on Saturdays were high points: cowboy shoot-outs, galloping horses, sword fights, Tarzan in the Jungle, Flash Gordon heading for Mars, the Mickey Rooney comedies and the musicals. The films and the books I read ignored or ridiculed people of African descent.

One great influence at Calabar was T.K. Wint, a physical training instructor. He had been a professional boxer and in 1918 was the undefeated Welterweight Champion of the West Indies. He fought in the U.S.A. and defeated the Welterweight Champion of Brooklyn at Yonkers in New York. He was well equipped to deal with troublesome teenage boys. When T.K. talked or smiled it sometimes seemed he was baring his teeth like a tiger. He had attended school in Cuba for about two years. Like many Jamaicans who went there, some of his front teeth were capped with gold. They seemed to glitter when he smiled. We ran, did calisthenics, ran again, learned how to make a proper fist and throw a punch. If you fooled around you would have to do extra laps.

But most of all T.K. talked to us about life; caring for your body, living clean and the dangers of sexually transmitted diseases. He transformed me into a muscle conscious health and strength fanatic. I grew more confident. One look of disapproval from T.K. slightly tinged with contempt, was enough to shrivel your macho.

As World War II dragged on, things like gasoline were rationed. Sometimes no gas was available for the few who had cars. People with money bought buggies pulled by horses. Some even had "coachmen." We smiled when we saw rich merchants clip-clopping down to their stores on King Street. Professional men like my Uncle Donald bought bicycles and rode to work, looking physically fitter for the exercise. Like a piano in the house, bicycles were a boyhood status symbol. Among the popular models were Hercules, Red Knight and Raleigh. I had a Hercules which was the majority favourite. We rode all over the place, even on the Palisadoes road towards Port Royal. With the sea on both sides, we imagined we were entering Pirate territory.

If you wanted to give someone "a lift" he or she would sit sideways on the crossbar (between the saddle and the handle) and be given a "tow".

My cousin and I once towed home two girls at midnight after a party. Another cousin (an overweight fellow) laboured far behind on his own. My fifteen year-old passenger became my first girlfriend. I wanted to impress her. With my arms around her as I gripped the handle bar, I felt like a hero, pumping ferociously up South Camp road from Sabina Park corner. I stopped at Cross Roads to allow my cousins to catch up. I pretended not to be tired. There was no one on the road at that time of night. When my cousins caught up they rested a little, and then we breezed through Half Way Tree and up Constant Spring Road to South Avenue. It is hard to believe now that Jamaica was so safe; past midnight on those dark deserted roads. And what a tremendous thing it was to be so full of steam and stamina, riding with your head in the clouds.

I don't remember being taught anything about Jamaica in high school. I discovered much later that the "School Authorities," embarrassed by the period of slavery, decided to deprive us of our history which in those days, and for long after, was seen as merely an appendage of British history. By sweeping everything under the carpet, they didn't have to grapple with some difficult questions.

We had classes in religious knowledge: Matthew, Mark, Luke and John, and the strenuous career of St. Paul. We learned Latin (Vergil, Livy, Julius Caesar, Homer, etc.) and became well acquainted with the Fall of Troy, the legends of Greece and Rome and the super human deeds of ancient Roman heroes. As a tribute to Greco/Roman civilization we had three houses at Calabar in my time: Troy, Rome and Sparta. I belonged to Troy.

The text-book I remember most was called "The Romance of Empire." The hard–bitten qualities of the ancients were attached to the equally hard-bitten British heroes who fashioned and maintained the wide-spreading net of Empire. I took it all into my tender, open mind, without analysis; Drake, Hawkins, Raleigh, Wolfe, Clive, Nelson, Wellington, Kitchener and Gordon, to name a few. "How can man die better than facing fearful odds," We were encouraged to become "Muscular Christians."

I got my last "licking" at age seventeen, for something I didn't do. The then headmaster was a burly clergyman from Australia. He made me bend forward gripping the arms of a chair in his study. He gave me six tremendous strokes. I can still hear the cane "swishing" viciously each time it descended.

What helped to save me was the controlled fury I unleashed on the football field, under the benevolent eyes of coach B.E. Phillips. He brought out the best in me.

Another teacher who brought out the best in me was Rev. Walter (Wally) Foster. He was a gentle man. On the day of his arrival in Jamaica, he played in a friendly football game on a team opposed to the one I was on. I knocked him down. He eventually married a Jamaican lady and became the headmaster at Calabar. I am sorry he is no longer alive. I would have liked to thank him again and also apologize.

The war came home to me when some of my friends joined the Royal Air Force (RAF) and began strutting around in the attractive blue-grey uniforms, before going off for training in England or Canada. Some who were Americans went into the U.S. Army, Navy, Air Force and Merchant Marine. My mother "put her foot down." She wasn't going to allow me to join the RAF. Uncle Billy was a little too old for recruitment. He went to England, hoping to join the British army, but was unsuccessful.

Every night we listened to grim news coming from the BBC. German Nazis were charging all over Europe, and their submarines were sinking vessels at sea. A ship coming from England in which three of my sister's friends, Lois Kelly, Vera Lawrence and Enid Edwards, was torpedoed. The three girls got into a lifeboat, but the davits broke as it was being lowered. They were dumped into the sea and were quickly hauled into another boat. But that one promptly capsized. Vera Lawrence and Enid Edwards were drowned, but Lois Kelly made it to a third lifeboat, and finally to a British destroyer.

The strange thing is that Lois Kelly (as she later said) dreamt the night before that the ship was torpedoed, and that Enid and Vera were drowned, which is exactly what happened. Uncle Billy was lucky. A torpedo grazed off the side of the ship he was on, and struck and sunk another ship in the convoy.

In the midst of all the war excitement I made the Calabar First Eleven Football (Soccer) team, to play for the prestigious Manning Cup. I acquired a reputation for being a pretty rough player, though not a dirty one. If the ball and an opposing player came my way, I was likely "to clear both man and ball." My position was right back, and the street boys called me "Dreadnought".

We went to Jamaica College to play them in the first round of matches. Michael Manley, later Prime Minister, was standing on the side lines in a crowd of Jamaica College Boys. He stood out because of his height. I had heard about him: the turbulent son of Norman Manley, Jamaica's most famous barrister. I was playing my usual physical game, and the JC boys were leaving the fields, we had to walk through them. They made tough, belligerent remarks, all except Michael. He just glared at me, as if he would have liked to do nothing better than to knock me off my feet. Calabar won the Manning Cup for the first time that year, in 1943.

On the following morning when the whole school was assembled in the chapel for the usual worship ritual, the team carried in the Manning Cup. We entered through the back door bearing the Cup as if it was the Holy Grail and we were veteran knights of the round table. Our chapel was at Old Slipe Pen Road; Calabar was an unusual place. At the far end in the altar section were two stained glass windows. If memory serves me right, one showed the good Shepherd holding a black lamb; the other showed Him with a white lamb. The chapel was where we learned hymns and sang them with great fervour. Noel Chapman and Lloyd Hall were among those who played the organ and I was among those who pumped it to keep the air going so the organ would play. On certain mornings we sat and listened to classical music played by the school orchestra conducted by Edward Gordon. On the walls were large pictures of two of King Arthur's Knights. I think they were Sir Gawaine or Sir Lancelot and Sir Percival. And somewhere was this motto: *"My strength is of the strength of ten because my heart is pure."*

We bore the Manning Cup down the long aisle to the section by the altar, where the headmaster and the teaching and other staff awaited us. At that moment the team rose to supernatural heights which were reserved only for great heroes.

One Saturday morning I went to JC to take extra lessons in mathematics from a teacher named B. St. J. Hamilton, otherwise known as Hambone. While I sat waiting upstairs, a group of boys in swimming trunks ran around the corner of the verandah headed by Michael Manley. He was bouncing what looked like a water polo ball as he ran. I envied them. They seemed so carefree and joyful, while I was about to struggle with problems presented by Hambone. The last time I saw Michael before I left Jamaica he was at Bournemouth swimming pool. He was playing a water polo match. His father, Norman Washington Manley, appeared on the scene. N.W. (as they called him) was wearing his characteristic three piece suit. But it didn't matter whether he looked smart or not; people stood in awe of him.

I had developed a keen interest in rough-and-tumble American football. I could pick up the college games on my radio, and on Saturday mornings, I sat 'glued' before it, lost in the football world. I knew the nick-names of the various teams, wrote down the names and physical statistics of the players and followed the fortunes of my favourites from week to week. My interest was fed by a superb sports announcer and commentator named Bill Stern. He used words like an artist uses colours. I could see the sky, the field, the spectators, the stalwart players, the marching bands. Bill Stern drew me out of Jamaica into whatever stadium the game was being played in. I wanted to play American football.

When I left Calabar I got a job as a temporary clerk in the Treasury. One interesting thing about the Treasury was that for the first time, a black man had been made deputy financial secretary and treasurer of Jamaica. His name was John Ebenezer Clare McFarlane, and he was a poet and author; a short, dignified serious–looking man with a goatee. Three of his sons had been at Calabar with me.

I shared a desk at the end of a long room with Tony Whittingham from Spanish Town. In between attending to the public I wrote and illustrated adventure stories. At lunch time, I usually went downstairs to the forecourt which was on King street, in the hope of seeing my girlfriend who worked nearby. One day I saw Bustamante standing on the piazza in front of the old post office. The Colonial government had locked him up in 1940 at Up Park Camp (the Military Camp) for nearly a year and a half, because of his relentless work in the labour movement. They thought he was a danger to "the War Effort". He was now the top man in the Jamaican trade union movement and had just founded a political party, the Jamaica Labour Party (JLP). He was about to run as a candidate in the first General Elections under Universal Adult Suffrage. His main rival was Norman Washington Manley, who also headed a political party, the People's National Party (PNP); which he had founded in 1938 at the time of the disturbances. These developments had made little or no impression on me.

The day I saw Bustamante on the piazza by the post office, he was wearing a tight jacket and a bow tie. His graying hair was almost standing straight up. His hands were in his pockets and he was rocking from side to side. People were pointing and saying:

"See Bustamante. See him there."

And Busta was chuckling.

As the time for the elections approached, some of us at the Treasury were recruited to work at polling stations. I wasn't old enough to vote. We worked until night, and had no trouble. I was conscious of all those coming to vote for the first time. I felt I had done something important.

One day my old friend, Derry Marsh, came through the Treasury in an Air Force uniform, to say goodbye. He looked very dashing. And then Donald Watler appeared in his uniform saying that the next time he saw me I would probably be married with children. That really knocked me out. I felt I had been left behind by my entire old bunch.

My sister Sadie, who was a little over a year older than me, had gone to the United States. She was now living in Washington DC, working at the British West Indies Central Labour Organization as a secretary to the director, Herbert McDonald. I think it was Sadie who came up with the idea for me to study at Howard University in Washington. I jumped at the idea. I applied to the university and was accepted.

My father thought I should study medicine. That was always the first thing people thought of in those "limited" days, as one of the few paths to economic success. My father, as a young man, had wanted to become a doctor, but had been unable to finance the venture. He had all the qualifications, was great at chemistry and physics and indeed, became a classic pharmacist. Those things turned me off, but I wasn't about to argue at that moment. I just wanted to get away. One of the last things I did before leaving home was to visit my grandfather, who had been so disturbed by Bustamante in 1938. My grandfather was ill and lying in bed; not looking at all well. For a going away present he gave me a suitcase and a small black covered diary. On the fly-leaf he wrote:-

"To my dear Grandson, with every blessing from God on you, and all your activities in the future."

There were two other entries:-

Sunday, January 28, 1945.

"Grandpa came to Kingston sick"

"Monday, February 5, Grandpa's Birthday."

I prized that tiny, black diary, and still have it.

Shortly after, with a feeling of being on the tip of my toes and on the edge of the world, I left Jamaica to study in the US. I began at once to record events in my diary.

This was before the coming of Rosa Parkes, Dr. Martin Luther King Jr. and the great American Civil Rights Movement. The Jim Crow era was very much alive and well in the US.

No sane person could even seriously imagine a phenomenon like Barack Obama. But nothing like that was on my mind. I was approaching the country of Razz-Ma-Tazz and might become a 'Football Hero', Razzle Dazzle, Razzle Dazzle, ZIP-BOOM-BAH. Robinson, Robinson, Rah, Rah, Rah--- TOUCHDOWN!

The Land of Razz-Ma-Tazz

When I landed at Miami Airport and went to the railway station, I saw a sign at a ticket-window marked "White," and a sign at another ticket-window marked "Coloured." The Jamaica in which I grew up was a shade-conscious society, rather than a racially divided one. A fine distinction, you might say. But deplorable as the "skin-shade culture" of Jamaica may have been, nothing in it struck you with such uncompromising force as those Miami signs.

At that moment, however, I wasn't really outraged. I was too excited and confused about leaving home and going abroad for the first time. So confused that I didn't realize I had a straight-through air-ticket to Washington D.C., which was my destination. So I went to the "Coloured" window and bought a ticket to Washington.

The train was segregated. They put passengers like me in a coach behind the engine. The dining car was at the rear of the train. At meal times we would have to wait until the "other" passengers had eaten, before being allowed to go to the dining car. I decided I couldn't fall in line with that practice, so I went without dinner that night.

I had never been extremely hungry in all my life. Life at home was firmly based on three square meals a day, plus afternoon tea on Sundays and snacks here and there, if necessary. I endured the pangs of hunger until lunch time the next day, then surrendered and joined the line trooping to the diner.

My sister had gone to the Washington Airport with one of her friends to meet me. She was worried for awhile when I didn't arrive on the plane. But being smart, she figured that her dolt of a brother had probably taken the train. So on the evening when the train was scheduled to arrive, she went to Union Station to see if I would show up. The train arrived in Washington about 9pm. I was amazed at the size of Union Station, and impressed by the crowds of people hurrying up and down. If Barnes, a young man whom I had met on the train, hadn't stuck with me I would have been lost. How could I have found my sister in that vast space, seemingly jammed with people?

I was standing with Barnes, looking around and wondering what to do when I heard my name being called on a loud-speaker. That was my introduction to a "paging system". My smart, experienced sister knew just what to do, though she was on the point of giving up. Barnes steered me to the place where the voice on the loud-speaker instructed me to go; and there was my sister, who stood five feet nine inches in her stockings. Was I glad to see her. I said goodbye to helpful Barnes, and, regrettably, never saw him again.

The Hungry Student

Sadie had booked me in at a men's hostel called Carver Hall, after George Washington Carver, the renowned African-American botanist and chemist. Sadie lived at nearby Sloe Hall, a woman's hostel or dormitory.

The Monday after my arrival I went up to Howard University to register. I was going to be a freshman. Again I was in the grip of Razz-Ma-Tazz. Movie memories flashed into my head: co-eds, cheer-leaders, football games, campus capers and proms. I was walking on air.

Sadie had been taking evening courses at Howard, and she was up on campus to make sure I didn't get lost. A very short, neat-looking man, wearing glasses and a hat came down a paved pathway towards us. Sadie greeted him and introduced him to me. "This is one of my professors, Dr. Eric Williams," she said. Dr. Williams shook my hand warmly and gave me a friendly smile. Little did I dream that I had just met the man who was to be the first Chief Minister, Premier and Prime Minister of Trinidad and Tobago. But at the moment he was professor of social and political science.

What struck me most as I rambled up and down the campus was how out-going and friendly everyone seemed. Greetings on every side:

"How you doing?"

"What you say?"

young men talk.

Inevitably, the Trinidadians brought their "fete culture" to Howard. Soon I was singing and dancing calypso: *"Ding-aling-aling-aling-aling-aling-aling-aling-alo...,"* whenever somebody put on a party in some basement or ill-lit place. Ken Tracey (otherwise known as "Dick Tracey"), his brother Ernest, Peter Chen, Cyril Josephs (who was a wrestler) and George (Nanton) Barrett from Sangre Grande were the chief practitioners and exponents of "Iron."

West Indians went in for track, and launched a soccer team. I felt that our American football heroes were a little disdainful of the game. I hoped to play at the position called end, so I could catch the football and run for touchdown. But the "wicked' coach threw me in the line at tackle. Even in the days before 300 pounds linemen became fairly common, a tackle needed to be very hefty. At about 195 pounds (on a slim and limited student diet) I wasn't really big enough for the position, and I didn't know how to watch for "dirty tricks." At practice sessions, when we wore no protective gear, some tough fellows who had just come out of the army, gave me a good mauling. I was hopping around with a "Charlie Horse" for a week or two, and had to take water therapy treatment at Freedman's Hospital. That put an end to my football career, but not to my interest in the game.

On the gentler side, I was very fortunate to meet Father John Burgess, the University's Episcopal Chaplin, who had started a Canterbury Club which I joined. It was 'everything good'. We had great meetings and put on socials, plays, picnics (at places like Rock Creek Park), and other really nice and wholesome events; quite in contrast to the calypso fetes. It was better than any fraternity or sorority, and we had a newspaper, the Canterbury Chronicle, which I gladly edited. I was president of the club for a while.

The only mistake Father Burgess made was when he tried to "twin" the club with Maryland University's Canterbury Club.

There were a lot of girls in the Maryland Club. After two or three very successful visits by the Maryland Club to Howard, the Maryland authorities quietly put an end to the project. In those days, Maryland was a segregated university. The Canterbury experiment was just too far ahead of its time.

In the first week of May 1945, news came that the German army had surrendered. I was now living in Cooke Hall on the campus and was in my room, struggling with class work. I was in no mood to celebrate.

On Thursday, July 3, I got a letter from home informing me that my grandfather had died. I was stunned, even though I knew he had been ill. A monumental part of my living background was suddenly gone.

Beyond the borders of Howard, we were well aware that Jim Crow was vigorously alive. Restaurants, cinemas, public transportation, night clubs and joints of all sorts, and even churches were segregated. We seldom if ever, went downtown. We felt we would be trespassing, and could be prosecuted. I was happy to have nothing to do with that scene. It was anti-life.

However, if you wanted a holiday job, it usually meant going on to the "Monster's" turf. Mostly, I worked washing dishes, glasses, cutlery and pots in restaurants; keeping dining rooms supplied with clean glasses, cups, plates, ice and rolls, helping the chefs in the kitchen; fetching food from the walk-in freezer, sending up orders on the kitchen elevator (the dummy). And after closing time, mopping out the kitchen and dressing rooms and wrestling heavy garbage cans up a ramp to the outside, to await the garbage trucks in the morning hours.

I also worked in warehouses, unloading things like 140 pounds flour bags from railway freight cars; it was dreadful. It was difficult to wash off all the flour from my face, arms and hands before taking the street car to go home. When I got home,

I would find small bits of water-mixed flour sticking to my face, and in my hair. What a sight! I can imagine what people on the street cars must have thought.

In those days I usually ate in sleazy lunch-rooms at the work site, in the company of the roughest labourers. Serious-faced men, some of them with hearts of gold. Once, while loading, I missed my footing and fell on my back in the opening between the platform and the railway car. A heavy sheet of metal we were using in the loading started to come down on me; but my work-mate grabbed hold of it and hung on 'til I scrambled free.

Perhaps the softest job I had was when I worked as a model for an art class on campus. They wanted to know if I would pose in the nude. I said *"no way."* Not with all those girls in the class.

I wore swim trunks. It was hard work. Sometimes I had to hold difficult poses for a long time. I got one dollar an hour. The worst job I had was in a run-down hotel. I had to sweep the sidewalk in the morning, do the floors, and double at the front desk to book guests.

It was best when we worked in restaurants. The hot shoppes were our favourites. We got a generous free meal and could 'engineer' snacks in between. We also got away with taking home ice cream after work. George (Nanton) Barrett gained about 20 pounds on one summer holiday restaurant job; drinking plenty of milk. I went up to about 205 pounds. Ernest Tracey was lucky. He got a job as a lifeguard at Banneker Swimming Pool. But under the influence of Sneaky Pete Wine, he went downtown one day and got beaten-up and jailed by cops.

But, we really didn't have to go downtown, except to places like the Library of Congress or to take a boat ride on the Potomac. There were enough cinemas, restaurants, snack places and juke joints around Howard; like "The Little Café" and "Cozy Nook." And the most wonderful thing about our university was that we didn't have a constant fight with rejections. Yes, we had the odd jibe, but it was really nothing. I had a lot of wonderful American friends: like Tree and Grady Welles, "Muscles" Maxwell and "Shoulders" Hargiss and "Pluto." We admired the student barber, whose name was Merriweather; and Shelton and his splendid orchestra, which rehearsed in the Cooke Hall basement, and sounded like Glenn Miller sometimes; and all those army veterans, some of them with scars, who came to Howard after the war: Sandy Green, Hank House, Hadley, McFarland, Zack, John Fitz-Gerald and Billy Pogue. Some like McFarland, had been in Patton's army. McFarland had had a fist-fight with a captured German soldier one day, and seemed to have come out as a draw. There was a grim-looking man named Hatton who had a bayonet scar on his chest. They were mostly a tough-looking bunch of giants; nothing like the stereotypes I had seen back home in films.

Not to be forgotten either was the wonderful ROTC contingent, with their marching exhibition on ROTC day. And the Howard Choir! Lord, could they sing! And the girls were like pearls and diamonds. Everybody seemed sharp and keen, dressing in style and making my Jamaican clothes look dreadful.

But over and above everything were my professors and lecturers: Alaine Locke, John Hope Franklyn, Rayford Logan, Leo Hansberry, Merze Tate, Sterling Brown, Summer and the 'respectable' Dr. Menes (so-called because he looked and sounded so very respectable). And how can I forget dear harassed-looking Mrs. Wilhelm, who struggled so hard to teach me German. Graduates of touted universities may keep their boasts, but Howard gave me something that was "quality", and also unique. The education was "open" and not embedded in ethnic assumptions and erroneous starting-points which were an assault on my humanity.

I left there feeling ennobled and liberated, but the question of Jamaica and the Caribbean had still to be addressed. In five years I had never had the means to go home for a holiday, not even for Christmas. Changes, largely unknown to me, were taking place; and certainly the narrow world out of which I had come was not something to return to. Militant Trinidadian students at Howard were arguing about self-government from colonial rule and some kind of Caribbean unity. But, in the repulsive face of Jim Crow, my British passport had become a kind of shield. And that was not a fashionable thought in militant student circles. I remember in the back of a street car one day an African-American student, whom we had annoyed, shouted at us:-

"who do you think you are, anyway. You're nothing
but damned British subjects."

I didn't take it as an insult. Back home, in my narrow colonial country, nobody would dare order us to sit in the back seats of public transport.

Matters came to a head for me one day, when Norman Manley, the eminent Jamaican barrister, came to address the students. I don't remember what he spoke about; something to do with Jamaica and the future of the British Caribbean. But I felt proud. No need to rely on that British passport as a shield any more; not as long as my country could produce a man like that. He answered all questions with the greatest ease, and with a marvelous command of the English Language. I guess Trinidad's Eric Williams, Professor of Social and Political Science at Howard, could have done the same. But it was Norman Manley who was on the platform that day, and he was a Jamaican. I felt I could back him against any world leader in combat.

Graduating And Going Home

The Japanese, allies of the Germans in World War II, surrendered in August, 1945. The next year my sister, Sadie, went to Chicago and got married to an old high school friend of mine, Bob Staples, who was in the U.S. Navy. That was about a year after my arrival at Howard. With Sadie's departure, the only prop in my immediate world was removed. No more Sloe Hall hospitality. Bread and jelly became the weekend stand-by.

My father was now on pension. Things were hard for him and he had to scrape and make enormous sacrifices to send my periodic cheques, which didn't always cover the necessities. My steady diet at the cafeteria on campus included spaghetti and meatball, chili con carne, pork and beans, hot dogs and beans, corned-beef hash, scrapple (cornmeal boiled with scraps of pork, then fried). My mother came to the U.S. and visited me in Washington. I had moved from Cooke Hall to Mrs. Milton's home at 524 Tea Street N.W. Mrs. Milton was on a list of house-holders who took in students. One of her rules was that no food must be taken to the room. But almost every night I secretly took home a pie (usually apple) and a quart of milk for supper.

One night, when I was walking home with my mother to Sloe Hall where she was staying, we stopped at a shop run by a Jewish family where I bought my pie and milk. I introduced my mother to the father and son behind the counter, and the father said to my mother. *"Lady, I have just one piece of advice. See if you can persuade your son to change his diet."* My roommate and I sneaked in jelly and bread at Mrs. Milton's, to fight weekend hunger, and hid left-overs on a ledge outside the window. The stuff was sometimes forgotten out there, and covered by snow. In spring, when the snow melted, paper bags with stale food would be revealed. Mrs. Milton would have killed us, if she had known. I soon abandoned my pre-med courses hoping my father wouldn't be too disappointed. The caged animals being used for medical experiments horrified me. Post-mortems would have been out of the question (my imagination was too vivid). Chemistry (which my father loved) turned my blood to ice water. Instead, I majored in history and minored in psychology. That gave me two options for the future. I graduated with my bachelor's degree on Friday, June 3, 1949, a fine spring day. Dr. Ralph Bunche of the United Nations (who was on the Howard Faculty from 1928-1950) and Madam Pandit (sister of Nehru) were special guests. I felt low, having no relatives in the large crowd.

When the time came to receive our diplomas I was shocked when my name was the first one to be called. I climbed to the platform almost in a daze and there was old Mordecai Johnson, President of the University, grinning at me and holding out my rolled-up diploma. Later I had my pictures taken in cap and gown.

I plunged into graduate work with history as my subject. I chose a topic for my thesis which I hoped would be relevant in Jamaica: *"George William Gordon and the Morant Bay Rebellion of 1865."*

I had learnt nothing about it in my school days at home. It was a fortunate choice. Eleven years later (in 1960) Jamaica's new Parliament building would be named after Gordon. Several years later he would be made one of the seven National Heroes of Jamaica.

I moved from Mrs. Milton's to a room in a house rented by Cyril Josephs, the student from Trinidad who was a wrestler and also the barber for a few of us. My room was badly heated, the blanket was short and my toes froze every night during winter.

My hard-pressed father sent me as much material as he could find on Gordon and the rebellion. I spent long hours at the Library of Congress in the city, which contained a great deal of material on the subject. Gradually I put my thesis together under the hard, constant scrutiny of the grim-faced head of the History Department, Dr. Rayford Logan. Then suddenly one day, Logan instructed me to submit my finished thesis for examination. The deadline was alarmingly close. Who would type it for me and what would it cost? Panic! Emily Johnson, the girlfriend of one of my Trinidadian colleagues, volunteered to help. She was a big-hearted girl from "down south." She had her typewriter. I bought paper and carbon and took them with my hand-written manu-script to her apartment. She started working almost at once. There was no time to lose.

The first two nights she typed until about four in the morning. I sat beside her, proofreading the typed sheets and "interpreting" my occasionally bad hand writing. She gave me dinner and snacks, and sometimes I fell asleep on the green rug in her room.

On the Wednesday night we stayed up until dawn. Emily gave me breakfast in addition to dinner. My oral examination was set for Thursday at 5pm, in a room in the library. I was very nervous as I waited outside. But when my turn came and I entered the room my nervousness disappeared. At the table were the "Big Guns" of the History Department: Logan, Lofton, Tate and John Hope Franklyn. I sat at one end of the table and answered questions. At the end of it, the "Big Guns" seemed pleased. I passed with flying colours. I hurried to Emily's place to work with her on the final thesis. Two friends, Dorith Tomlinson (a Jamaican girl working in Washington) and Ruth, whose surname I can't remember, had come over to help Emily, so she could get some much needed

Emily

sleep. That night we worked again until dawn and finished the job. I handed in the thesis on Friday afternoon.

When I went to Emily shortly after, with all the money I had, hoping it would be enough to meet her charge; she flatly refused to take a cent. I was dumbfounded. It was again time to make arrangements for a cap and gown.

Friday June 9, 1950 was Graduation Day. It was a very hot day. I was gripped by terrible misgivings as the departure time approached. But a shift had already taken place. Several of my friends and colleagues had left. I was becoming a "venerable" veteran in a sea of fresh new faces.

Dewey-eyed girls hypnotized by my appearance, had mistaken me for all sorts of things. One girl, seeing me poised on the edge of a swimming pool, thought that I must be the son of a chief from some Pacific Island. At a dance one night, one of my partners impressed by my muscular appearance, said: *"you must be a Football Hero!"* A female history lecturer, seeing me dressed in a waist-long leather and fur jacket, lounging among a group of fellows in a passageway, approached me and said: *"you must be Air Force."* I was truly sad at having to disillusion her.

The most ridiculous thing in this "Alice In Wonderland" period happened during a summer school. Some girls (they may have been part of a sorority) were putting on a sort of water ballet at Banneker swimming pool. They wanted a guy to flex his muscles while they danced around him to a popular song which said:

> *"O he's got a fine brown frame, I wonder what could be his name, etc."*

Somehow I got roped into the event. I stood, self-consciously at the edge of the big pool in my swim trunks, doing various muscular poses while they danced about me in their skimpy bathing suits to the singing of "Fine Brown Frame...."

At the end of the number I dived into the pool with a mighty splash and swam a lap. Somebody in the crowd of spectators shouted:

> *"well what do you know; the guy can actually swim!"*

for the rest of that summer, whenever I passed some girls on the campus, they would sing: *"O he's got a fine brown frame..."*

But now, I was on my way out of that youthful paradise, where I might be any wonderful thing. When those gates did close behind me, Howard would become a treasure house of my life, illuminated by the girls who had mystified and enthralled me, the cheerful striding macho-boys and the demi-god professors and lecturers, who had made me feel important. In later years, projections from that Treasure House would appear before me like film and video clips.

The thought of leaving was painful, for I loved Howard. It had become my second home, the place where I grew up in so many ways. I remember my first sight of snow. I was studying in the library when Basil Keane, a fellow Jamaican, ran inside in a state of great excitement and said: *"it's snowing."* I went outside and stood in the gently-falling white flakes. Pure magic. If it were possible to remain frozen in time, that is the one moment I would choose. And maybe also the winter night when, at a late hour, I danced at a prom at the law school, to Nat King Cole's Christmas song *"Chestnuts Roasting on an Open Fire"*.

I didn't want the music to end. Some people at home warned me to stay away from Jamaica. My Uncle Billy encouraged me "to come." A month or so after graduation, I packed my things and took the train for Chicago, to spend some time with Sadie before heading home. I slept in Sadie's front room, wrote short stories and worked at a couple of jobs. I was a delivery truck helper. I worked in the large, gloomy warehouse and factory of the Chicago Curled Hair Company on the night shift: 11pm to 7am.

I wrestled down huge bales from mountain stacks, cut them open, and fed the contents (some kind of mattress filling) to a conveyor belt. It was back- breaking.

I went on picnics, swam in cold Lake Michigan, attended parties, played tennis and rowed about in a lake at one of the public parks. But it was all delaying tactics; putting off the day of departure. Then I met a Chicago girl who was rash enough to think that getting married to me was a good idea, even though I was soon to depart, had no job, and no immediate prospects. We came out of very different worlds, and scarcely knew each other.

I took an Eastern airlines flight out of Chicago on March 2, 1951, changed to a Pan-Am plane at Miami, the next morning, and took off for Jamaica. Some returning Jamaican Farm workers were on the plane. There was no Air Jamaica in those days. When I arrived at the Palisadoes Airport (now Norman Manley International Airport) I recognized relatives in a crowd behind a wire fence: mother, father, uncles, aunts and a couple of cousins. I had taken up occasional pipe-smoking, in imitation of some "Cool Cats" at Howard and my respected English Lecturer, Sterling Brown. Pipe smoking made me feel dreadful. It was a great day when I was able to throw away my pipe collection. But on the day of my arrival, the biggest pipe I had was stuck between my teeth. I was still sufficiently immature to think it made me look "cool." I arrived alone, leaving my newly-acquired wife to follow shortly. I hoped to get a job before she arrived.

If someone had told me I would never see Dick and Ernest Tracey again, or Peter Chen; hearing the merry clang of barbells in their company, I would not know how to believe it. I did see big Joe the wrestler, when he came to Jamaica as a member of a touring team of wrestlers. He spent a night at my home. "Nanton" Barrett ate a meal at my house with his Norma from Texas, but the three Clarke brothers from Tobago disappeared from my radar screen. Of the old Canterbury Club American regulars only Catherine Hagler who got married to Jamaican Frank Roberts came into my world again. Father John Burgess visiting them in Jamaica pulled in a good crowd of graduates for a memorable evening. And that was it.

Mocho And Busta

My mother was running a guest house in Mocho, Clarendon. I don't recall that there was any electricity or running water at the time. I stayed there with my mother for nearly three months, mostly helping to clear a piece of land she had bought. I went to Kingston several times, hoping to find a job.

One night the legendary Alexander Bustamante, then Chief Minster of Jamaica, arrived at Mocho. He usually stayed at the Guest House when he was in the area, and my mother knew him well. He loomed out of the bright moonlight, a man of tremendous physical presence. He climbed the steps, strode from the verandah, through the living room, into the dining area, talking all the way in a curious sing-song voice; a loose-limbed, fair-skinned man with long grey hair, (which was not as wild-looking as when I first saw him years ago). He had strange, challenging eyes, and I guessed he was six-feet three or four. I found myself standing tall, as if to measure against him.

My mother was excited. She introduced me to Busta. *"This is my son,"* she said proudly, as if that was supposed to mean something to him. His secretary, Miss Longbridge, was with him. We sat and talked, I mostly listened. I didn't know how to relate to Bustamante. I found him disturbing. He was too masterful. His challenging eyes seemed to expect submission. But I had just come out of a Jim Crow environment and submission was far from my mind. Bustamante sat at ease at the lamp-lit dining table in the Mocho night. My mother was much impressed, but gazing at his challenging eyes, beneath the thick eyebrows, I didn't quite understand that I was in the presence of the Chief Minister, revered by the majority of the Jamaican working people.

My wife arrived early in April: my mother prepared a feast of welcome, dominated by a roasted pig. My wife was coming from her native Chicago by way of Kingston. I was apprehensive. From a big power-house U.S. city, she found herself in deep Mocho, without electricity, running water or telephones. And on the lamp-lit dining table, a whole roasted pig, head and all, waiting to be eaten. It was a sight she had never seen and she was very tired. The roasted pig was standing in a big dish "on all fours".

I took my wife up to my mother's hillside land, to help fork, shovel and throw stones; plant grass and feed animals. The Mocho folks smiled when they saw her going up the road in blue jeans and straw hat, with a hoe or cutlass; sometimes getting wet in the rain. At the house we got water from a big tank. When it rained we took a shower outside, under an overflowing gutter which caught water from the roof. At night we read by lamplight. No radio.

Bustamante came again at about midnight on May 23 and woke up the whole house with his loud voice. He left early the next morning.

The days passed and in August, my wife and I took a bus to May Pen to see the Denbigh Agricultural Show. We returned in an ancient bus, which was fine down hill, but when it started to climb a hill it shuddered and stalled. The driver then backed downhill a bit and stopped and asked the men to get out. They cheerfully obeyed. Apparently they had had the experience before. The driver revved the engine, and powered the smoking, struggling bus towards the top of the road. Some men ran behind and pushed, as it went grinding up. When it reached the top and came to a halt, everyone cheered. Then we got in and drove off.

Not long after this, my mother gave up the Guest House and we went to Kingston in an old truck, packed high with furniture and other household things; I rode in the back, perched on furniture, along with a truck-man or two. My wife rode in the front, squeezed between my mother and the driver. We had two punctures and a few break-downs, and didn't reach town until one in the morning. It had taken us about seven hours.

We stayed with relatives and friends for about four days before finding a suitable place to rent. One night my wife and I came home late from a movie and were locked out of the house where we were supposed to stay. Fortunately, we found space in the home of an acquaintance, but had to sleep on the floor. I can't imagine what it was that sustained us in those days.

Getting A Job

Getting a job began to look impossible. I was soon tired of walking around with my jacket over my arm. Then one of my aunts introduced me to Evon Blake, editor and publisher of Spotlight News Magazine, and Theodore Sealy, editor of the Daily Gleaner. The Gleaner was then on Harbour Street, and as Jamaica's foremost newspaper, seemed the better place to find a job.

My aunt went to the Gleaner with me. We climbed well-worn wooden stairs to the second floor, and entered a large open room, which was the editorial office. It was full of mostly grim-looking men working at desks. Theodore Sealy sat like a Sultan at the back of the room, facing the entrance. He could see every-thing. He was a thick shouldered burly looking man with a large head; hard eyes, a tough face that offered no comfort. I was placed in a chair beside him. *"What can you do?"* he asked. *"Well,"* I said, somewhat surprised, *"I can write."* After a few questions about my academic career, he said: *"suppose you don't get a job here, what will you do?"* I paused, again surprised by the question. *"I guess I may have to think about going back to America."* At that moment, strange as it may seem, the thought filled me with dread. What had become of my shining dream-land: The land of Razz-Ma-Tazz!

Sitting to Mr. Sealy's right was a short, thick man Mr. Sealy introduced him as Percy Trottman, second in command of the editorial staff. I was told to come back on Monday morning.

On Monday morning I arrived at the Gleaner before nine o'clock. I was early so I walked to the waterfront and looked at the warehouses and the sea. Everything seemed so "primitive." I sat on a clean place on the side walk and watched mule-drawn drays and men lounging about. At 9:50am I went back to the Gleaner Office. Trottman wasn't there yet. He arrived at 10:30am. I guessed he had worked late the night before. His face was as tough as Sealy's; noncommittal. He could have been cast as (what was called) "a Heavy" in a gangster movie.

"I want you to go up to Mona, to the University," he said, *"and get a story"*. The University of the West Indies was in its infancy. There was nothing much happening when I got up there. I wandered about the wide, open expanse of Mona land, looking at several long, narrow wooden buildings in which refugees had been housed during World War II. I wrote a story on the library, went back to the Gleaner, typed it, and then handed it to Trottman. While he was reading it I couldn't tell much from the expression on his face. He looked like a man who had read too many stories over a great many years. But apparently the story was alright. I was hired as a trainee reporter and the story was printed.

The Editorial Crew

Jack Anderson, a veteran reporter, was assigned to instruct me in the fine points of newspaper reporting. He didn't seem too happy with having to "nurse-maid" me. He was a tall, burly man who tended to growl rather than speak. There were legends about the spectacular brawls that he sometimes had with the editor.

I couldn't help feeling I was somewhere back in the nineteenth century. Perhaps it was the ramshackle building and the general glum countenances; scrooge- like, straight out of Charles Dickens. There were a few young fellows who were not yet glum: Dudley (Bobeye) Byfield, Plump Ricketts, who covered the waterfront and died while I was with the Gleaner, and Nash, who was a sub-editor.

Gertrude Sherman, who had won a beauty contest, had a terrific smile and was a rose among thorns. At first she sat behind me, back to back. One day she said something to me which I didn't hear. So she doubled her fist and punched me hard in the back.

George Daley, the Crime reporter, was short, chubby and moon-faced. Baz Freckleton, in Sports had a serious look and sometimes a fixed stare. Vic Reid, the brilliant up-and-coming novelist, wore thick-rimmed glasses and always seemed to have a pipe in his mouth.

Consie Walters, Charlie Balfour and Raymond Lewis already had that "Newspaperman's look" a seasoned, late-night earnest. Hector Bernard and Calvin Bowen, a "Mutt and Jeff" tall and short duo, seemed sophisticated and arrogant. Ulric Simmonds, the Political man, appeared like a corsair: rakish, dangerous-looking, neat and compact. "Strebor" Roberts (Strebor was simply Roberts spelled backwards) was broad and powerfully-built. He reminded me of my friend at Howard, Cyril Josephs, the wrestler from Trinidad. Strebor's formidable head appeared to be carved from some hard substance. His neck and shoulders were thick. Horse-racing was his specialty.

Alva Ramsay, dropped in now and then. A striking, white haired, patriarchal looking man. He had a no-nonsense face and tennis was his specialty. His wife, Ivy, was a champion tennis player. Commercial radio had just come to Jamaica (RJR) and Alva Ramsay was one of those 'mystical beings': a radio commentator.

Percy Miller was an agricultural specialist. He had worked with many news outfits such as Public Opinion, Jamaica Times and Spotlight Newsmagazine, and had published a journal called Caribbean Post. He had a gentle short-stepping walk, his head held slightly to one side. He seemed to be looking through you into far distances and there was a dream-like quality to his eyes.

Cliffton Neita, was a round face man who wore spectacles through which peered intelligent eyes. He looked like a solicitor of the Supreme Court of Judicature. He came in now and then.

Facing Percy Trottman, was Trueman; a blunt, inscrutable countenance, concentrating on his notes and the typewriter before him. Nearby was paunchy Jack Harris, large-eyed, just off the streets, still in his jacket, and dictating to a typist.

On the Northen side where Strebor Roberts and Alva Ramsay sat, was Ferdie Williams, who always looked harassed and unhappy. Along the western wall, to Trottman's right, were some ancient Titans; venerable, ponderous, "Father B" (Barton) and heavy-eyed, heavy-voiced Martin Smith, who looked like a cross between a judge and a headmaster.

On my second day on the job, I went with Jack Anderson to the criminal courts. For lunch I had two patties and a milk shake at a "dump" off parade. The next day I visited a civil court and almost fell asleep. Then over to a criminal court in the afternoon, where the famous, diminutive barrister, Ethelred Erasmus Adolphus Campbell, was arguing a case.

On Friday Trottman sent me to the criminal courts again and instructed me to come back with stories. I made notes all day and at about 4 pm, went back to the office and typed my stories. When Jack Anderson read them he exploded. I had duplicated some stories he had just written. When he cooled down he criticized and corrected my stories and showed me how to head them up properly. I retyped those that needed doing over, handed the lot to Trottman and went home; very late. The next day, to my great surprise and pleasure, one of the stories came out in the paper.

Junior Journalist

If memory serves me right, my salary as a trainee reporter was four pounds, or four pounds ten shillings per week. I lived with my parents so I was able to manage, but things were hard on my wife. She had to deal with a tough mother-in-law.

I sat beside Jack Anderson, who kept on overseeing my work. One day a report came in that someone had been murdered at Palisadoes. A man named Whoppy King was arrested. It was alleged he surprised two lovers on a lonely section of the Palisadoes road at night, raped the girl and killed her lover.

I was sent to the Sutton Street Court to do a story the day Whoppy King was brought there. There were policemen on either side of him. A man in plain clothes was behind, he also looked like a police officer. There was excitement inside the court. I was standing just outside the door of the court room. Whoppy King and the guards stopped right next to me. I had a good look at him. He was a short, powerfully built man. His shirt was partially open and I could see his muscular chest. He looked dogged and desperate, like a trapped animal. He made some blood-thirsty remark and then they took him into the court room.

I hurried to the Gleaner and wrote a story which appeared the next morning on the front page. Vic Reid added something to it but I didn't mind. As far as I was concerned it was my story and it had made the front page. Shortly thereafter, my pay went up to five pounds per week.

My Gleaner Days

My Gleaner Days

On August 17, 1951, news came that a very strong hurricane was going to hit Jamaica. The meteorologists had named it Charlie. There had been a hurricane in 1944, but I didn't remember much about it. My wife (Lor) had never experienced a hurricane. We stood on the verandah, outside our bedroom door, to watch the hurricane come.

We heard the wind approaching, roaring from the distance. We marveled to see limbs being torn off trees and to hear the rain coming in on the wind. A stray dog which hung around the yard ran under the house. The telephone line from the street snapped. The wind shoved us. Something dark was hurling towards us. It was no longer fun. We hurried inside and bolted the door.

No light. The electric wires had gone down. The roof shook and leaked. The walls seemed to tremble. Water came under the door and through a transom. Soon our bedroom was under water. We went into the dining room and saw my father struggling to keep the back door from blowing in. My mother was trying to help. We got a day bed and backed it up against the door. That helped. The wind howled and shook the house, as if trying to beat it down. Water was everywhere. We were terrified and felt helpless. After a while we were able to endure everything, especially as the house was holding up. We stopped being afraid. Lor and I fell asleep at about 2 or 3am, after the worst had passed.

Hurricane Charlie destroyed about ninety per cent of the island's bananas. Fruit trees and other crops were severely damaged. At least one hundred and fifty-four people were killed. Thousands were homeless. Many took shelter in schools. A large number of churches had been blown down. Kingston was in shambles. People were in a bad mood, trying to figure out who to blame for the wreckage and how they were going to manage.

The newly arrived Governor, Sir Hugh Foote and his wife, Silvia, were visible. The crisis gave Governor Foote an opportunity to show his energy, concern and goodwill for the people of Jamaica. He came out of it like a knight in shinning armour.

We could hardly get out of our house. The streets were blocked by fallen trees and all kinds of debris. There was no water. We went around with containers trying to find water. On September 4, it appeared that another hurricane was heading straight for Jamaica. People battened down and waited fearfully. But the hurricane veered to the south, and only a little wind and rain came.

I examined my bank book and found I had managed to save twenty-two pounds. Better than nothing. Getting to work was hard after the hurricane. One morning I waited nearly an hour for a bus. A man came up in a buggy and offered me a lift. His name was Webb. Our speed going down was about the pace of a subdued canter. But we reached Parade without being overtaken by a single bus.

To make life more interesting I began writing short stories, hoping to get them published in the Gleaner's Wednesday Magazine. The first one came out on October 3, a memorable day. I wasn't supposed to be paid but they gave me a guinea (one pound, one shilling) for each one published. My favourite was "Small Time Jones," based on an adventure of our crime reporter, the elf-like George Daley.

After awhile, Mr. Sealy took me off the streets and assigned me to sub-edit at the Country News desk. Then he sent me to the "Headline" section presided over by the night news editor, who had just returned from a course in the U.K. and had taken an instant dislike to me, resulting in a couple of clashes.

I was so grateful to breathe what I thought was the free air of Jamaica that I didn't realize I was an oddball. John Maxwell later pointed out to me that I was the only university graduate in the Editorial Department. My speech had been influenced by my years of immersion in the U.S. Evon Blake was stunned by what he called my wife's "flaming hair." A well-known literary lady stopped me on Harbour Street one day and berated me for marrying a foreigner. And I was still so naïve as to walk in to the Editorial on one occasion with my largest pipe stuck uncomfortably between my teeth. I was a sitting duck oddball.

The night news editor didn't hide his dislike for me. He had a deep "frown line" between his eyes. Working with him was the worst thing that happened to me at the Gleaner. He always glared at me and snarled, and literally chucked the work at me. It was a relief when he took a day off and big, silent "Franco" Francis took over the chair. I got a break when Baz Freckleton went on a cricket team to Barbados for two weeks, and I was assigned to work at the Sports desk with Strebor Roberts. One day I covered five cricket matches.

Some journalists cultivated a tough image. They hung out at such downtown "watering holes" as Moby Dick, Captains Cabin and Sloppy Joe. There they relieved the daily pressures and exchanged information and gossip. In the old days reporters were regarded as a fairly-low form of animal life. When they went to the seat of Government (then at Headquarters House, 79 Duke street) for news, they had to go around to the back gate and pick up prepared hand-outs. But things changed significantly as the self-government movement progressed. Men like Stephen Hill Sr. and Theodore Sealy gave stature to the profession. Alva Ramsay and Strebor Roberts were fountains of wisdom in their particular fields. Ulric Simmonds, the political reporter acquired "important" contacts. But it was for "growling" Jack Anderson that I felt affection. Many years later I was genuinely grieved to hear he had been shot dead by a house-breaker. I guess "fighting" Jack had tried to tackle the intruder. Fresh faces appeared in the ramshackle Editorial Cavern. Bertram Collins and Derek Walcott (students at the new University College of the West Indies) came in for summer holiday jobs. Some forty years later Walcott (from St. Lucia) would become the Caribbean's first Nobel Prize winner.

Barbara Goodison (now Gloudon), John Maxwell and Sybil Campbell joined the staff. Barbara was pretty, energetic and engaging. John was a nice school-boyish lad, quite serious for his age. You would never think they would become such formidable spokespersons in later years. Sybil was bright and attractive and would go into the Foreign Service.

There were two noteworthy drivers at the Gleaner, both connected to the entertainment business. One was an ex-comedian called Racca, who was one of a duo know as Racca and Sandy. In the old days they were among the best of several duos which did comedy skits at such places as the Ward Theatre. I don't know what happened to Sandy, but Racca was now just a tired sleepy-eyed driver, waiting to transport staff. He looked like anything but a comedian.

The other noteworthy driver was "Caledonia" Robinson, a part-time night club M.C., who was still very active. The name Caledonia came from a song he loved to sing. It was a kind of signature tune. At some point in his act the audience usually called on him to sing it. *"Cal'donia, Cal'donia! What makes your big head so hard?"*, and with a mighty shriek ("yeah!") Robinson would leap high in the air and come down in a split on the dance floor, to the roar of the audience. The first time I saw him do it I was afraid he would hurt himself. But he was up in a flash, yelling: "But I love her, love her just the same. Crazy 'bout that woman 'cause Cal'donia is her name." And split again, to another roar from the audience. Caledonia Robinson usually performed at red-hot Club Havana, along with accomplished Rumba dancers from such places as the Dominica Republic and Cuba, who provided a dangerous spectacle.

To save car fare for other purposes I sometimes walked in the hot sun from police station to police station (if they were not too far apart). Duty Officers would run down the list of "happenings" in their log books (robberies, wounding, rapes, killings, domestic disputes, etc.) and help me decide what was worth reporting. Clerks at the courts briefed me on the more interesting cases. I was well treated. Every now and then I would buy somebody a drink out of my travelling allowance (to keep my sources).

Hellshire And The Jamboree

I got a refreshing break at the end of January 1952: a two-day assignment with a wealthy businessman, James Gore, in the Hellshire area. We left the Yacht Club on the motor cruiser "Invader" at 8am, arrived at Wreck Bay before lunch and swam in the crystal-clear water. Burke, the photographer, was also on the assignment. The beach was clean and white. We walked over ragged, rocky land and visited the ruins of "Morgan's Castle" after lunch: then spent the night aboard the "Invader" at Wreck Bay.

The next morning I got up early and went on deck to begin writing my story. The water was green-blue-grey. The sun came out of the sea, on the horizon, like a huge orange ball. It sent a trail of light over the water. When we had come into the bay the day before, I had seen sharks swimming around. Aboard the cruiser with James Gore was his son (Big Jim, who kept crocodiles) and an American lawyer. Mr. Gore had this dream of developing Hellshire, which was then just a barren waste, with honey-combed rocks and iguanas and wild pigs.

We sailed from Wreck Bay to Manatee Bay, in search of crocodiles; caught a little one and killed a big one. Leaving Manatee we headed for Coquar Bay, being overtaken on the way by a 'school' of porpoises which frolicked before the boat. The following day, Saturday, we visited Pigeon Island, Big Half-moon Island and the Pelicans; then headed home.

Four days later, on February 6, King George VI died. Princess Elizabeth became Queen and I wrote a sentimental (corny) piece

51

about the King's death and the succession from the perspective of Queen Victoria's statue, then at South Parade. The Gleaner published it. My three stories about the Hellshire trip, together with Burke's photographs, were also published. I felt as if I was getting somewhere.

The first Caribbean Jamboree was opened on Wednesday, March 5, 1952, at Briggs Park on the eastern edge of Up Park Camp. The Star newspaper, decided to put out a daily supplement (The Jamboree Star) to cover the event in depth. I was one of the main "work horses." Sybil Campbell was another. I was virtually on my own. Eric Dawson, veteran press photographer, was assigned to take the pictures. I was lucky to have had him to work with. He was mature, affable, and encouraged me.

We tramped all over dusty Briggs Park, visiting the sub-camps where scouts from various countries were quartered. The sub-camps were named after historic British figures: Nelson, Rodney, Benbow, Drake, Raleigh, Hawkins, Penn, Venables and Henry Morgan. Presiding over the Jamboree was the Chief Scout of the Commonwealth, Thomas Godfrey Polson Corbett, Lord Rowallan, a tall, lean, craggy-faced Scotsman. There were scouts from the U.K., Guyana, St. Kitts, Antigua, Montserrat, Bermuda, the Virgin Islands, Canada, the U.S.A., Cuba, Panama, Barbados, Venezuela, Curacao, Honduras, Trinidad, the Cayman Islands, and Haiti.

Governor Foote and Chief Minister Bustamante were among the VIPs who visited the camp. After fifteen days it was all over. I felt good about the part I had taken, and kept all the copies of the Jamboree Star. In April I got a ten shilling raise, bringing me to five pounds, ten shillings per week. We had moved out of my parents' home and were sharing a small house with friends.

Kitchen space was a problem. My wife had to cook simple meals on the face of an electric iron. So the raise in salary made it possible for me to buy a cute little oil stove for twenty-two shillings and sixpence. I now had fifty-eight pounds in the bank, still a long way from owning a house or car.

Evon Blake And Michael Manley

E von Blake, editor and publisher of Spotlight News Magazine, came to see me. He had read my stories and liked them. He offered me a job: 350 pounds a year to begin with; roughly 64 pounds more than I was earning.

Mr. Blake was a thick-set man of average height. For a brief period he had been a policeman, but now he was a successful, independent journalist with a hard-hitting style. He was noted for his attacks on colour prejudice, and was most famous for his "daring deed" at the Myrtle Bank Hotel. Myrtle Bank was one of Kingston's major luxury hotels. People of dark complexion were not welcome there as guests. In fact, Blake hired a newly-arrived Englishman who was able to become a "member" of the Myrtle Bank, but Blake couldn't get membership.

One day he walked into the hotel, "bold as brass." The swimming pool was full with people of the "right complexion". Blake put on a bathing trunk and before anyone could stop him, he dived into the pool. There was an instant shock-wave of horror. When he surfaced, almost everyone was scrambling to get out of the pool. There was a great furor and much embarrassment all round.

When the story of Blake's deed was published it caused a great deal of outrage. They were demands for an explanation and denial. Something that had been known all along and tolerated suddenly crashed.

So that was Evon Blake, a self-confident, self-made man, who wore his hat rakishly, cocked to one side, and always seemed to have a pipe in his mouth. In fact, he clamped down so hard on his pipe that his teeth had worn away on the side which held the pipe stem. I accepted his offer of a job and he gave me a contract. I sent my resignation to Mr. Sealy on Saturday, May 24. He wrote a very nice letter of recommendation, which said:-

> *"Mr. Carey Robinson who served for a short while on the Editorial Staff was considered by us to be very promising material for the profession, was well mannered, disciplined and capable. We regretted when he decided to leave us."*

It seemed the nicest thing anyone had ever said about me. I was pleasantly astonished, for Mr. Sealy had usually seemed so hard-faced and indifferent. Maybe his newspaper man's cynicism was merely a facade he had carefully cultivated.

At Evon Blake's Spotlight I interviewed and wrote stories on a lot of prominent people: politicians, business people, professionals, artistes, theatre personalities, etc. But it was soon obvious that it was going to be a dead-end. It was a small organization. No career path was possible. There was only room at the top for Evon Blake. His whim and fancy guided the course of the magazine. There was a practical necessity to court powerful business houses which could buy advertising space; the well-being of a mere writer like myself was of little consequence. I soon began to look for another job. Near the end of November or early in December, I wrote to the newly established Radio Jamaica, applying for a job as an announcer.

Sir Winston Churchill, Prime Minister of Great Britain, arrived for an official visit on the evening of January 9, 1953. On Saturday, January 17, just about everybody in the Corporate Area of Kingston and St. Andrew went downtown to see him.

He sat on an elevated seat in the back of an open car, and gave the familiar V for victory with his fingers which he had made famous during the war. He was seventy-eight but his face appeared cherubic and unlined. The crowds cheered wildly as his car rolled by. The bus I travelled home on that evening had a hard time maneuvering through the mass of vehicles.

Michael Manley had returned from the U.K. and had joined the staff of the Public Opinion newspaper. He came to the office to see Evon Blake. I was typing a story in my office near the back of the place when I heard someone running down the passage. Michael appeared in the doorway, holding the door frame and leaned in, with a big grin on his face. "Hi" he said in a warm voice, as if we were long lost friends. He came up to my desk and leaned on it and we talked for awhile. He spoke about his parents with great admiration and without embarrassment. He seemed so frank and open. Then he breezed off and was gone. Our paths were to cross several times in the future.

Louise Watts, a friend of mine (wife of an old Calabar schoolmate) was working at Radio Jamaica. On January 20, about three days after Churchill's departure, I got a message from her to get in touch with Mickey Hendricks about the announcer's job I had applied for. He told me to come in the next day for an interview.

I had been living on my nerves, swallowing anger, anxiety and frustration. The prospect of changing jobs again and entering a brand new field brought on stomach pains. I knew I could write, but could I speak well enough to hold on to an announcer's job? For the rest of that day and the night that followed, my stomach gave me hell.

The following day I went to Spotlight early, got a jacket I had left there and headed for Radio Jamaica. I remembered once seeing people gathering there to be interviewed; a long line stretching from the gate to the entrance of the building. Would such a line greet me now? But when I walked through the gate in my jacket and tie, up the pathway and into the building, I was the only person there.

Archie Lindo came down the passageway to meet me. He had been in broadcasting since ZQI days. He took me to a studio and we sat at a table, facing each other, with a microphone between us. Archie asked me why I wanted to be a radio announcer. I don't remember what I told him. He put two prose pieces before me and told me to read them. One of them had to do with classical music. I made a couple of pronunciation errors which he corrected. Then I was taken upstairs to be interviewed by Mickey Hendricks (who was the sales manager) and by the "Big Boss" himself, William MacLurg, the managing director. The last time I had seen tall, large-eyed Mickey Hendricks was when he was acting in Shakespear's Midsummer Night Dream, as either Demetrius or Lysander. His father owned a furniture company, lived in a black and white mansion near the corner of Hope Road and Old Hope Road and was a product of privileged Jamaica.

William "Bill" MacLurg was a very different character. Born in England, he had been educated at the Royal Academy of Music and the Royal Academy of Dramatic Art in England. He had worked as a studio engineer and in the Drama Department of the BBC; then in the Empire Department (Overseas Service), the Home Service and finally, the Variety Department of giant and very influential BBC. During World War II, he served for four and a half years with the RAF until he was seconded to the Army to help on the British Forces Network. After the war he returned to the BBC, but quit about a year later and joined Overseas Rediffusion Limited. In 1947 he set up Trinidad's first broadcasting station. He came to Jamaica in 1950 as Radio Jamaica's Managing Director.

MacLurg's face was as tough as Sealy's, but he had a well-modulated almost gentle voice, quite in contrast to his steely eyes and small, hard mouth. He was the type of British Imperial figure found in every corner of the empire, in positions of authority. Every inch of him reflected that intimidating image. Above all he was a trained and experienced broadcaster in the traditional sense and his standards in connection with spoken words were high and demanding. Nevertheless he allowed a lot of room for experiments in programme production.

That morning at Radio Jamaica, I was on a different planet from the newspaper/magazine world, but the journalistic skills I had acquired were to prove very useful.

MacLurg and Hendricks wanted me to start the next day. I asked them to give me until Friday, the day after. I would have to persuade Evon Blake to break the contract and let me go. I would be on probation at Radio Jamaica for three months, during which they could kick me out at any time if they felt like doing so. It was a hard decision, but I had already made up my mind. The job at Spotlight was depressing me. Blake was no easy man to deal with. I kept on wondering why "older guys" in positions of authority found it so hard to be considerate to younger subordinates. Was it a hang-over from the old whip-wielding days? When I asked Blake to waive the contract he said: "no." I offered to get someone to take my place. He still said: *"No"* I was desperate.

Fortunately, Irene McGann a young Englishwoman, who was Blake's secretary and who was sympathetic to my plight, came to my aid. She persuaded Blake to let me go.

I was enormously relieved and phoned Archie Lindo at Radio Jamaica to say I would take the job. It was agreed that I should start on Monday, January 26. There was at least one thing for which you had to give much credit to Evon Blake. His shocking dive into the hallowed waters of the Myrtle Bank pool had done as much as anything else to crack the wall of silence and acceptance of the pernicious shade/colour prejudice, which had for too long crippled and distorted the Jamaican society.

The Glamorous (Vanished) World Of Radio

There was only one radio station in the island: Radio Jamaica (otherwise called RJR). Everybody listened to it.

In that connection, M.G. Robinson (an employee of Radio Jamaica) told me this rather funny story. During hurricane Charlie in 1951, the staff laboured heroically throughout the long, horrible night to keep the station on the air, in order to maintain contact with listeners. Electric and telephone wires were down all over the place, but the "heroic" radio workers thought nothing of this as they went about their tasks. Afterwards, as near as they could figure, there had only been one listener to their broadcast: a person with a rediffusion set, whose line, connected to a telephone pole, had survived the hurricane's fury. Their well-intentioned efforts had been in vain.

Since there was only one station, if you were a radio announcer you quickly became a celebrity; a "household name." You took on an aura of importance far in excess of the reality. You were identified in the public mind with the Razz-Ma-Tazz and star-glitter. All the big-name orchestras, singers and soloists, people who appeared in Hollywood films, rubbed off on you: Glenn Miller, Artie Shaw, Tommy and Jimmy Dorsey, Benny Goodman, Louis Armstrong, Dizzy Gillispie, Duke Ellington, Edmundo Ross, Count Basie, Harry James, Ray Anthony, Percy Faith, Melachrino and Mantovani, Oscar Peterson, George Shearing, Nat King Cole, Bing Crosby, Frank Sinatra, Rosemary Clooney, Doris Day, Billy Eckstine,

Eddie Fisher, Elvis Presley, Mario Lanza, Mel Torme, Tony Bennett, Ella Fitzgerald, Sara Vaughn, Billie Holliday, Perry Como, Judy Garland; and one could go on, and on, and on; names that mean nothing now to most young Jamaicans.

The radio announcer appeared to be intermingling and co-existing with all those stars. Judging by your voice and style, listeners conjured up an image of you. The human senses are great deceivers, and listeners were free to imagine anything they wished. Girls and mature women fell in love with a voice. Sports commentators acquired an exaggerated importance as they brought their judgement to bear on test matches and international sporting events.

At the Gleaner, the editorial personnel tended to resemble the mass of Jamaicans. To paraphrase the words of one prominent latter-day politician, if you put them among the people (especially without their jackets and ties) you couldn't tell the difference. With the announcing staff of Radio Jamaica however, it was the opposite. At the time I went for the audition there was only one "black" face to be seen among announcers. That belonged to a Canadian of Jamaican parentage named Fred Wilmot. And he was only part-time, a freelancer.

I don't think this state of affair was deliberate. Unlike the "blood sweat and tears" journalistic atmosphere of the Gleaner, Radio Jamaica gave the impression of being an elitist organization, and it simply reflected the traditional culture of the day. Banks, insurance companies, hotels, stores, some clubs and numerous private sector organizations were also in the tradition. Except for Wilmot, the announcing staff could have had easy access to the old Myrtle Bank pool. And even technical staff (wedded to very practical matters) tended to be of the same persuasion. One notable exception was M. G. Robinson, who was the studio operator during most of my training sessions.

But the situation was about to change, rather rapidly. A young Canadian named Allan Rowe, who had a fine voice, was assigned to "take me in hand."

I began by reading from an "exercise brochure." In the afternoon I sat in Studio Three with Karl Magnus and Merrick Needham, for about three hours, watching and listening. Maybe they were trying to impress me. I don't know. But they worked very well, facing each other on either side of a "two-way" microphone; alternating commercials and programmes. I was impressed.

I had to spend hours in the record library, learning where various types of recordings were filed: classics, jazz, religious music, military bands, sound effects, popular songs, choirs, themes and incidental music, BBC and CBC transcriptions, calypsos and mentos, semi-classical music, operas and operettas, country and western, children's music and stories. Numbering records according to the card catalogues and learning how to "build" programmes and type a programme sheet.

Of most importance however, were the reading exercises with Rowe in the operator's booth. I learnt how to keep the log containing the programmes, commercials, newscasts and time signals that made up the day's schedule. I went down in the evening to see what happened on the late shift and did station breaks (this is Radio Jamaica and Rediffusion) which were heard by my family at home. After that I sat in on the morning shift with Brian Arscott. The following day I went on the air for the second time during the frequency change at 5:45pm. The next day (Saturday), Archie Lindo told me to take off Sunday and start Monday morning on the "Coffee Club." That night I killed thirty-one mosquitoes in the kitchen at home. Yes, I actually counted them!

My colleague announcers were an interesting lot. You got to know people more intimately at RJR than at the Gleaner, perhaps because you had to work so closely together, for hours, as part of a team.

Archie Lindo had been a station manager at tiny ZQI, the place where broadcasting started in Jamaica. He was also a poet, playwright, author and elocutionist. Perhaps because he was an elocutionist, his style was rather "careful."

Roy Lawrence, the sports authority, was a burly six-footer with a deep scar on his forehead (from about the hairline, to one eye-brow) which gave him a dangerous look. It was easy to imagine that he got it in some terrific fight, but it was due to a medical operation which hadn't come off very well. Largely because of his cricket commentaries he was well-liked throughout Jamaica. He was also notorious for, what might be called, malapropisms, or faux pas. When describing the arrival of Governor Foot and his family at an event, he is alleged to have said.

"Now here comes Sir Hugh Foot, Lady Foot, and the little feet." And: *"Sir Hugh is taking off his foot* (instead of "his hat"). And while narrating the progress of Queen Elizabeth at a function, from an elevated vantage point, Roy is supposed to have said: *"and the Queen is walking under me now."* Another time while reading an item of sports, he is alleged to have said: *"the batsman made ten runs, nine of which were singles."* But whether true, or only half-true, Roy's occasional "lapses" only served to further endear him to his admirers.

When faced with an error on a script, Roy might not "argue" with the offending word. Consequently, when reading a narration about the inscription on the Statue of Liberty, instead of saying: *"Give me your tired, your poor,"* he read what he saw before him, which was: *"Give me your tired, your POOF."*

Karl Magnus was a "Puncher" with a breezy style; always trying for "the big sound." He was a fierce competitor who never hesitated to "pull your leg" when you made a mistake, especially while reading the all-important news.

Merrick Needham was small and trim but had a mighty voice. He possessed a strong British accent and his diction was impeccable. Merrick came across best at ceremonies and state occasions. He was big on protocol and correct forms and usages.

Brian Arscott had six daughters and he liked to sing (or croon) like Bing Crosby, the American super-star. Brian would sometimes open the mike and sing-along while some famous singer's record was being played. Somehow he got away with it. We called him "Crooner B." Many years later, after he had migrated to Canada, he wrote me to say that, after six daughters, he had finally had a son.

Valerie Bolton was a daughter of Harold Warner Bolton, lawyer and spokesman (Polo Club, Jockey Club). She had long black hair and an "exotic look."

Dennis Gick started in the old Seaview Avenue days with Archie Lindo. A tall, gaunt, stoop-shouldered, chain-smoking Englishman, he was a freelancer, and had a deep, dignified voice that was great for classical-music programmes and ceremonies.

In my estimation at the time, Fred Wilmot was Mr. Super Cool. As a freelancer he did Luncheon Date at around midday, and Saturday Matinee, which was all about jazz. If you were any kind of a radio listener you tried not to miss Fred's shows. His relaxed and easy manner made listening a pleasure. And he knew his jazz and all the great Jazzmen like Charlie "Bird" Parker, Bud Powell, and Lester Young.

Fred Wilmot was so self-assured that he seemed cocky. He was a reformer; caught up in the drive to liberate colonies. In Kenya, an Independence movement had begun, which involved the Kikuyu tribe and Jomo Kenyatta (who eventually became head of the country). A dreaded militant faction called the Mau Mau had arisen out of the Kikuku. Some Britishers were killed. The British launched a major offensive to suppress the Mau

Mau, the Kikuyu and the Independence movement. There were acts of terrorism and violence on both sides. Hundreds of Kikuyu were slain.

Fred Wilmot wrote an article for Public Opinion Newspaper where he worked, saying that if what the Mau Mau were doing was wrong, they had his sympathy.

There was an immediate reaction. It was said that the Colonial Secretary called a top-level meeting at Headquarters House on Duke Street, which was then the seat of Government. The subject of the meeting was Wilmot.

The next day, when Wilmot went to Radio Jamaica to do Luncheon Date, arriving about five minutes before broadcast time, as was his custom, he found Archie Lindo in the chair in the studio. Archie, with tears in his eyes told him to go upstairs and see "Mr. Hendricks." When Fred entered Hendricks' office, Hendricks said: *"You are fired. You will never broadcast in Jamaica again."* The Star newspaper ran a big headline: WILMOT FIRED! His photograph was used along with the story. For the first time most people were seeing what he looked like. Because of his accent they had thought he was a "white Canadian." The editor of Public Opinion was advised to fire him, which he did not. When Wilmot's fans heard what had happened they were furious. A group gathered outside Radio Jamaica and almost tore down the fence. When it was clear that he would not be on the Monday night show he had been doing, there was a public outcry. Hendricks phoned Wilmot and almost begged him to come down and do the show. Wilmot roughly refused.

Rumour had it that there was a move to deport Wilmot as an undesirable. When he went to the regular weekly press briefing at King's House, his colleague journalists ignored him, after the meeting he asked the Governor, Sir Hugh Foot, if he could speak to him. When the others had left and they were alone, Wilmot asked if there was any truth to the rumour that he was to be deported. Governor Foot looked him squarely in the eye, a hard "Colonial Official look," and told him he knew nothing about such a thing.

Looking back now, it all seemed like "a storm in a tea cup," but it was an indication of the times, and of the hold that "favourite" broadcasters had already achieved.

I must also mention Ken Maxwell, who left Radio Jamaica to head the Government Broadcasting Service shortly before I arrived. Ken, an Anglo/ Jamaican, had a comic touch. He had served with the armed forces in Britain during the war, and loved to fool around with the Jamaican dialect. Years later he assumed the role of a dialect character called "Pro Rata Powell," and had listeners chuckling over his humorous patois monologues.

Along with Ken Maxwell was an Englishman named Leslie Murray-Ainsley, who was in charge of Schools Broadcasting. Schools Broadcasting did a very good job, even though Murray-Ainsley's "upper-class accent" and choice of theme music, gave it a decidedly British flavour, which seemed a little out of sync as Jamaica approached independence.

There were many Chinese, or people of Chinese extraction, working at the station; mostly girls. I don't know why this was so, but they had a reputation for efficiency and hard work. There were a couple of horrid English types in Engineering and the Rediffusion Division. Radio Jamaica was running a campaign at the time to increase the number of Rediffusion subscribers. Rediffusion was a wired relay system through which radio signals were distributed to specially constructed rediffusion sets. These sets were rented out and could only pickup Radio Jamaica. Lascelles Anderson (a new announcer) and I were chosen to go around in a van fitted with loud-speakers, to encourage people to subscribe. The van was going into the humbler areas of the city, among poor folk. When Lascelles and I asked the Englishman in Rediffusion why we were chosen and not any of the others, he bluntly told us, it was because of our colour. The spirit of Jim Crow rose up clearly before me as I looked into his calculating, insensitive eyes.

One weekend I went to the station, got the keys to the library and began "building" a programme. A telephone call came for me at the front desk and I ran out to get it. The keys fell from my pocket as I raced down the passage past a newly arrived British chief engineer.

"Come back here and pick up those keys," he bellowed, as if he was the Lord of a Manor and I was his serf.

There was Wally Matthews, an Englishman and an engineer. Wally was unassuming, quiet, gentle, friendly and helpful. He was one of those expatriates who would stay on in Jamaica, throughout all the changes that would take place. He got married to a fine-looking, elegant Jamaican girl of Chinese extraction.

As far as I was concerned, it was a happy day when tall, husky Douglas Webb was made Rediffusion manager. He was a Jamaican who had served in the RAF during World War II, and his hobby was flying. When the new Boscobel airstrip was being opened in 1954, he was warming up a single engine Cessna 170 to take some friends for a spin. Suddenly Chief Minister, Alexander Bustamante, hurried out of the main body of spectators to ask Douglas if he could take him up, so he could have a look at Tower Isle and Ocho Rios from the air.

Douglas said, "yes," and took off with the Chief Minister and his secretary, Miss Longbridge. It was a twenty-minute flight, and all the way, he was acutely aware of the tremendous responsibility he had taken up; flying the Head of Government in an unscheduled flight in a single-engine Cessna 170.

Under Douglas Webb's management, the number of Rediffusion subscribers shot-up from 3500 to 7000 in eight months.

Bill MacLurg

MAN AT THE TOP

Bill MacLurg, the man at the top with the eyes of blue steel, was a puzzle. MacLurg was a hard smoker, like Dennis Gick; but unlike Gick he was robust and seemed healthy.

One morning I encountered a song with a French title on my music sheet: "Darling Je Vous Amie Beaucoup", sung by Nat King Cole. Not knowing any French, I "butchered" the title. The next thing I knew, Bill MacLurg was in the operator's booth, looking at me as if I had just committed cold-blooded murder. He must have flown down from his office.

He disappeared from the operator's booth. The studio door opened and there he was, like an angel of death. He came around the table, stood beside me and pointed at the music sheet. Very deliberately, he pronounced the title in what to me sounded like perfect French.

"If you are going to keep this job," he said, in a voice as cold as ice, *"you'd better learn to pronounce words in foreign languages which you come across in your scripts."*

If you had taken a whip to me I couldn't have been more humiliated. But from then on I had a most healthy respect for foreign words. If I couldn't handle them I found a way to leave them alone. Fortunately for me, I knew some Spanish and German.

The RJR Strike

The management of the station sent out an order one day, that announcers would be trained to operate the studio equipment. That upset the operators. They felt that their importance to the organization would be underminded. I don't remember for sure, but I think this was when the union (the Bustamante Industrial Trade Union –BITU) really got into the place. A poll was taken and the majority voted for the union to represent them. I had "good" friends among the operators and I cast my vote. The junior managers weren't happy about that.

One day, while I was on the early evening shift, I announced a record and signaled the operator to play it. Instead, he cut off the microphone, waved at me and left the operator's booth. The operator was Arthur Hassan. He pushed the studio door open and told me they were on strike.

There was pandemonium, a lot of scrambling to try to get the station back on air. The strike didn't last long. The operators got their wish. The order was withdrawn. But it was only the beginning of things.

Thursday, June 4, 1953, a couple of days after the Queen's coronation, was my day-off. I thought I could take it easy; because I didn't have to worry about catching the bus to get to work. The telephone rang. The station was calling. There was a strike on and they wanted me to come at once.

When I got to the station I found that, of the 104 members of staff, at least 75 were on strike. The only people I saw in the building were the senior engineers, the executive staff, the announcers and a couple of clerks. The management was determined to fight the strike. Engineers were in the operator's booth in the studio, acting as operators. They weren't very good at it, and production was rough. A lot of mistakes were being made. I worked 'on air' for three hours.

The next day, the engineers started training Roy Lawrence and Karl Magnus to operate. The strikers hung about outside the gate in hostile groups. They heckled me as I walked past them. But I was in no position to join them, even if I wanted to.

As the days passed the strikers got more hostile. Staff members who were still working, but had no cars, were provided with transportation by the management. Police were on duty at the station day and night. The last few days had been wet and humid and that made things more depressing. I, and at least one other member of staff, still came in on foot. That meant going through the crowd of angry strikers and enduring their harsh words and curses. Some of them I had got along with very well, like Lawson the librarian, operators Donaldson and Benie King and George Hamilton a driver. It was depressing to see them giving me ugly looks. I hoped the whole thing would soon be settled.

By Sunday, June 7, the operation in the studio was becoming smoother with fewer mistakes. The ironic thing was that the unrest had started with a protest against an order that announcers would be trained to operate the studio equipment. Now, because of the strike, announcers were being trained to operate, to help keep the station on the air. Things would never be quite the same again.

In spite of the intermittent showers, strikers continued to picket the gate. But they were growing desperate, grimmer and more truculent. On Tuesday, one of the executives, Mr. Austen, an Englishman, was driving through the gate. His car touched Lawson, there was a shout of protest. Lawson struck Austen in the face and knocked off his glasses. That night, a lot of Rediffusion wires were cut. I had to open the station the next morning and we had a very difficult time getting on the air. The management now thought it necessary to provide me with transportation, to and from work.

The next day was a holiday; the Queen's birthday. I had the day off. There was a lot of marching to and fro downtown, with Governor Foot taking the salute. On Saturday, I did my first 'Disc Jockey" show; doing both operating and announcing. It was "Saturday Matinee", Fred Wilmot's old show. I worked from 1:00 to 5:00pm and found it much more exciting and interesting than just plain announcing. Of course, it was very exacting and required greater concentration.

Things went on this way, with desperate strikers still hanging about outside and non-strikers like myself labouring very hard inside and getting better and better at what we were doing. On Thursday, June 18, management sent out notices of dismissal to all strikers, and announced that vacancies now existed for staff in the company. I don't believe anybody seriously thought that things would have gone that far. The loss of jobs couldn't be taken lightly. There was no other radio station in Jamaica.

The union would have to do something at once, otherwise it would lose 'face'. Mr. Hugh Shearer came to the station, striding confidently and smiling, but somehow looking dangerous. I think this was my first sight of him close-up. From what I can remember he had a long meeting with the management, behind closed doors. Not too long after, the strike was settled and I believed most of the staff returned to work. But things were never quite the same again. Hard lessons had been learnt.

We had moved back into my parent's home and once again, my wife and my mother had reached 'the end of the line'. My wife had not been able to get a job and I still wasn't earning enough to make it permanently on my own. So, amid much weeping, my wife packed up and departed for Chicago.

Her plane left at 4:30pm. I wasn't able to see her off because I was doing the "Saturday Matinee" shift and couldn't get anyone to substitute for me. But my Uncle Billy turned up at the station and kindly went down to the airport to be with her, until her flight left.

I had to draw out practically all my savings to send my wife back to the U.S. Five days after she left, I got a letter from Bill MacLurg, informing me that I was getting a raise in salary of six pounds per month. The other announcers also got a raise.

One night I went into the front yard and shouted at the overcast sky; begging the Creator to show me what to do.

RJR's Lively "Live" Programmes

All the "veteran" announcers had cars. One or two were quite ramshackle-looking, but they moved and that was the important thing. I didn't have a car, so the odd working hours made life quite difficult.

The early morning "Wake up Jamaica" show and the late shift ending with the "Live Wire" show, presented special problems. Either the bus hadn't yet started to run when I was ready to go to work, or it had stopped running when I was ready to go home. The "Wake Up" show signed on at 5am, except on Sundays when opening time was 6am. The "Live Wire" (heard only on Rediffusion) came on after 'radio' signed off, and ended at 1:00am.

For the early morning show I got up at around 3:00am, had breakfast and started walking briskly: Dumbarton Avenue, along Molynes Road, through Half Way Tree, down Maxfield Avenue, hoping to be overtaken by a bus (and if no bus), I walked along Lyndhurst Road until I reached no.32. The best I can say is that all that exercise helped to keep me healthy. I just couldn't afford to be late. The roads would be dark and empty and dogs would come out at me sometimes.

But it was while walking home one night after the "Live Wire" show that I had a most frightening experience. There was not a soul around. My footsteps sounded loud on the asphalt road. As I was passing by the St. Andrew Parish Church Cemetery, about to go down Molynes Road, a white dog suddenly rushed out of the

RJR Staff 1955-1956

cemetery, through the fence and right across my path, just missing me. I jumped with fright and surprise. My heart raced. I could feel my hair standing on end. I never saw where the dog went. It just vanished. Needless to say, I never walked that way again at that time of night.

There were several "request" programmes attracting a tremendous amount of mail. Some names, or nick-names, turned up on just about every programme. One lady called herself "the Vision of Loveliness."

If fans found out you had a preference for something they would send you a lot of it. At one time they called me "The Peanut Vendor" because it got around that I liked peanuts. The next thing I knew I was getting loads of peanuts. Too much to handle.

A lady name Pansy, who sang on an amateur talent programme, sent me a fruit cake. The next day (Constitution day) was a holiday. I had no food in my room. I was hungry, so I took a chance and ate cake all day.

As early as 1950 (shortly after Radio Jamaica was set up), a programme called "The Adventures of Morgan Henry" went on the air, as RJR's first live programme. It came on at 8:45 on Sunday nights and was sponsored by Captain Morgan Distilleries Ltd. (makers of Captain Morgan Rum). It starred Ranny Williams, who was then regarded as "Jamaica's most popular theatrical personality."

Ranny wrote the scripts and his character was called Morgie, "a shiftless rascal," whose chief desire was to eat all the food he could find, and "wash it down with Captain Morgan rum."

At first it was a monologue, but after about three months, Alma Hylton (later Mock Yen), a young up-and-coming actress was introduced as Putus, Morgie's wife. Other characters were added. Versatile Ranny doubled for all the male parts except one which was played by Archie Lindo. Equally versatile Alma doubled for the female parts. All the characters were comical and rather "daffy." Another RJR success was the "Lannaman's Children's Programme", done in the big studio with an audience of specially invited children who sang and recited. Dorothy Hosang was the hostess. Later, when Cynthia Wilmot (Fred Wilmot's wife) joined the programme, she wrote scripts, and the children acted out the dramatizations of fairy stories. After awhile, children wrote in and asked to be allowed to come on the show. One little girl pulled a surprise when she boldly announced that she had come to sing. She then belted out a popular jazz classic, to everyone's delight.

After Dorothy left, Valerie Bolton did "Lannaman's". I took over from Valerie and enjoyed being "Uncle Carey." The well known musician George Moxey, played the piano. I sometimes sang along with the kids.

I got a talent fee and that was most welcome. My bank account was beginning to grow. I was not happy when after about three months, our Canadian Programme Director Charles Richardson, informed me that Dorothy Hosang had returned to Jamaica and would again take over "Lannaman's".

Talent Parade

"Talent Parade", sponsored by Colgate Palmolive, was a big plus for Radio Jamaica. It started in 1950 on the stage of what was then the Tropical Cinema on Slipe Road. Essentially a singing competition, "Talent Parade" attracted a wide cross section of people. Contestants had to have strong nerves and a thick skin. The very enthusiastic audiences were merciless. If they didn't like a singer they would make it known in no uncertain terms. On the other hand, if a singer pleased them, they "brought down the house" with cheers and thunderous applause. The audience, both cinema and radio, wrote down their choices for each night's show and on the strength of that, contestants were either eliminated or went on to the semi-finals. After a group of six programmes, semi-final winners advanced to the final, where specially selected judges chose the "Champion."

The first "Talent Parade" ran for six months, every Tuesday night. It was tremendously exciting and ended on April 10, 1951. Audley Bailey was declared the winner and received a trip to Canada and a watch. The semi-finalists also got prizes.

The next series was held at the Carib Cinema in Cross Roads. After that the show moved to the big concert studio at RJR. Most of us took part in the show over time, as MC or commercial reader: John Phillips (Canadian), Mickey Hendricks, Hugh Wilson, Archie Lindo, Roy Lawrence, Merrick Needham, Fred Wilmot, Karl Magnus, Brian Arscott and I. When Brian took over as MC I read the commercials.

In the earlier days George Moxey and his band accompanied the contestants. But now we had "smiling" Baba Motta and his group, including Roland Alphanso on saxophone and Ken Williams on drums. We had such stars as Mercedes Kirkwood, Barbara Hylton (Alma Hylton, Mock Yen's sister), Blossom Lamb, Don Gallimore, Cecil Lawla, guitarist Janet Enright and Jimmy Tucker "the boy wonder." Songs such as "Because God Made You Mine", "Faith Can Move Mountains", "You'll Never Walk Alone", were enormously popular. When Brian Arscott wasn't there I ran the show with Merrick Needham's help. I did alright, and when Coca Cola decided to sponsor a talent show they asked that I do it. It was called "The Uncle Carey Amateur Talent Show."

The Green Austin

May 17, 1954 was a great day for me. I made out a cheque for two hundred and twenty pounds to Mr. Wesley Hewitt, for the purchase of his car; a green, 1949 Austin A 40. Mr. Hewitt turned over the keys and papers to me that night and I turned over the cheque to him. HALLELUJAH!!

After my wife left I had set a goal to buy a car and perhaps a little house before she returned. It was a very ambitious aim. Much of the talent fees I earned went into the bank. Sometimes talent fees for a month could be as much as my basic salary.

It was my old friend Derry Marsh who told me about the car. I couldn't drive so I left the Austin at Derry's place on Beechwood Avenue, near to Mrs. Gabay where I used to have lunch. M.G. Robinson taught me to drive. I started lessons the next night after I bought the car and actually drove home, with M.G. beside me. M.G. drove the car back to Derry's place that night.

Driving home whetted my appetite. I hated the thought of having to take the bus the next morning. The following night, after the late show, I drove along Palisadoes Road to the airport, with operator Lloyd "Red Dust" Chin beside me. Everybody already wanted to borrow the car; all the night-owl operators who had girlfriends to take out after dark.

I got my big red L (Learner's licence) and drove all over the place, especially at night after work, spending a lot of money on gas. Finally, on June 7, I took and passed my driving test, after a near miss with my front wheel on my third reverse. I took my mother to the airport eleven days later, so she could fly off to visit my sister Sadie in Chicago. On the way down the avenue into the airport's compound I got a flat tire; my first experience of one. My mother and father (who had come to see her off) walked the rest of the way. I couldn't get the car jack to work, but some airport men lent me a jack. I took off my shirt, changed the tire and drove in to the airport, shirtless and streaming with sweat.

About two and half months later my wife, Lor, returned to Jamaica, after an absence of a little over a year. I was very happy to go down to meet her in my own car, second-hand notwithstanding. She came off the plane carrying an Elma sewing machine in a green case and was the last one to come through the customs. It was so very satisfying to cruise along the Palisadoes Road, the two of us alone in my Austin A40. Except for my father we had the house to ourselves, with my mother being away.

Transition

General Elections were held on Wednesday, January 12, 1955. I voted for the first time. Radio Jamaica began carrying the results after 7pm up to 2:30am. When I went to bed, the fight was close: PNP 15, JLP 14.

In the morning we got the final results: PNP 18, JLP 14. For the first time since Jamaica got Universal Adult Suffrage in 1944, Bustamante was out of power. It had been a long, hard road for Norman Manley, but he was now the Chief Minister, the top man. He looked positively radiant as he took office on February 2.

Bustamante wasn't at all pleased, but he went into opposition with his head high. Radio Jamaica did an outside broadcast from the Denbigh Agricultural Show. During the platform speeches at the official opening, Bustamante appeared at the far end of the field. He was dressed in a black cut-away coat, with striped pants and a black top hat.

Attention turned away from the dignitaries on the platform. Everything was "put on hold, as Bustamante walked deliberately across the field all alone, straight and tall, as if he had just been elected Prime Minister of the Empire. Cheers went up, and Busta gracefully doffed his hat as he headed for the grandstand.

That year, Jamaica officially celebrated what was called "three hundred years of Association with Britain. The word "Association" was a euphemism; a pathetic attempt to re-shape history.

My daughter was born early on a Monday morning in September 1955. I was on duty at Radio Jamaica with a young announcer named Ian Richards. A call came from my Aunt Dorothy to say that *"things looked like they were about to happen."* It was 7pm. Richards said he had to leave at 8pm. He had a dinner party to attend.

I left about 7:20, dashed home and took my wife to the hospital. I left her there with my aunt at about 7:45 and raced back to the station. Thank God for the old Austin A40. My head was in the clouds, although I had hard thoughts about Richard and his dinner party. When my shift ended at 11:05, I raced back to the hospital. My wife was in labour. They let me into the room for a while and then suggested I wait outside. The baby was born at 12:30 am., beautiful. Not a wrinkle on her face. The next day I went to Steel's Restaurant, on East Queen Street and celebrated with a lovely meal of liver and onion. It costs me three shillings and six pence.

Uncle Billy died about a year later, after an operation in London. He was only forty-three. His powerful body had been undermined by diabetes and malfunctioning kidneys. Up to the age of twenty-one he neither smoked nor drank. But failure to complete his medical course at Edinburgh University, followed by a career on isolated land settlements and sugar estates, propelled him into a destructive lifestyle. It was a common belief in those days that smoking and drinking were manly pursuits.

A real man must be able "to hold his liquor" and blow smoke rings. Unfortunately for Uncle Bill he also married a lady who was "on the rebound". The death of their only child at birth (strangled by the umbilical cord which was around its neck) just about finished Uncle Bill. But to the last (and even to this time of writing), he was revered by those who knew him.

Top Talent

My last memorable break at RJR came in 1956, when Colgate Palmolive returned to sponsoring a major talent show. They wanted something different from the old talent parade. I was asked to come up with a new format. So I put together a series, using mostly talent from the old parade days, with comedy thrown in. The show was called "Top Talent". I wrote the theme song and the scripts, assembled the cast and directed each programme. Fred Wilmot was MC and sometimes the "straight man" Ranny Williams (of the Morgan Henry show) was the main comedian. Music was supplied by the Baba Motta Trio. The Frats Quintet (one of the most accomplished singing groups ever produced in Jamaica) was the main-stay singers. Special guest artistes included Totlyn Jackson, Marie Clayton, Mercedes Kirkwood, Lois Kelly and Alma Hylton (Mock Yen).

I used all kinds of situations, including cowboy stuff, wrote new words to well-known songs, (from current popular favorites by singers like Frank Sinatra, to selections from operas such as Figaro).

In the midst of things, Mickey Hendricks reminded me that the "Eddie Fisher" show came on at 8:30, right after "Top Talent". He didn't want us to pale by comparison. I took this to mean that so far, we were a least holding our own. When all the projected programmes had been broadcasted, I thanked God for the Talent fees I had earned. Then, to my surprise, Colgate Palmolive re-newed the contract for another "Top Talent" series. So, it was back "with my nose to the grindstone."

In addition, I had to do my regular shift in the studio, other sponsored programmes and assist in editing long speeches to broadcast length. Michael Manley came in one afternoon while I was editing a speech he had made. His new wife, the former Thelma Verity, was with him, a beautiful, charming girl. Michael still had his fresh, youthful look, disarming you with his grin, even though he was getting to be a hard-nosed trade unionist.

About this time I had bought a piece of land in a moderately priced sub-division. We were still living in my parents' house, my mother was back in Jamaica and things were beginning to heat up again. While I was at RJR, Lascelles Anderson, Adrian Robinson, Roy Reid and Dwight Whylie were among those who joined the staff. Lascelles became very popular. He played the piano on the "Lannaman's" show for awhile and later migrated to the United States.

Adrian had an authoritative voice and dressed casually. My nick-name for him was "the Tourist". This proved rather prophetic, for, in later years he not only became Director of Tourism, but also Chairman of the Jamaica Tourist Board.

Roy Reid had a rich, deep voice and was at the time a member of a singing quartet. His favorite song was: "Do do do, Mr. Parney do, I will make up the case with you", etc. My nickname for him was "Mr. Parney." Roy migrated to the United States and disappeared in the maw of the Big Apple (New York City).

Dwight Whylie had a cool and pleasant style and would become one of the many general managers of the Jamaica Broadcasting Corporation, which was to be set up in June 1959. There were also several non-Jamaicans who joined the announcing staff. Al Ponman, a tall rugged Canadian with a powerful two-fisted voice. Peter Orr, a lanky Englishman who was a Cambridge graduate (he eventually got married to Muriel Campbell, one of the daughters of Jamaican born Sir Charles Campbell who went back to live in the U.K.).

Canadian Charlie Babcock, the "Cool Fool with the Live Jive" (he was very popular and also married a Jamaican girl, a beauty named Betty Holtz). Brim Brimble from Canada, part-time sports announcer and commentator (a burly man who looked like a lumberjack). Barry Davis, a short, chubby Englishman and a trained musician (he was choirmaster at Kingston College at one time and he too married a Jamaican girl).

For a station without competition, I was struck by the heavy reliance on Canada and Britain for staff in the Programmes Department. Most of them were fine, reliable people and good at their jobs. Nevertheless, it was an indication that we were still very much in our infancy, as far as broadcasting was concerned.

An almost similar dependence was displayed when the Jamaica Broadcasting Corporation (JBC) came into existence in 1959. Other microphone personalities in my time included: Jean Capstick, Beverly Kelly, Joy Brandon, Alma Mock Yen, Margarietta St. Juste, Gloria Clarke, Harry Vendryes, Don Taylor, Desmond Elliot and Tina Barovier's mother, Violetta de Barovier Riel, with her "Listen Ladies" programme.

Government Public Relations Office

In spite of the notoriety and the opportunity for highly creative work, I began to feel that it wasn't going to be enough. We could make people laugh and feel happy, play their favorite music and give them some news, without any disturbing analysis. But, in a country that was rapidly moving towards full internal self-government and independence and which understood so little about itself, much more than entertainment was needed.

I read in the newspaper that there was a vacancy for an "Assistant Government Public Relations Officer". Norman Manley had set up a Government Public Relations Office to inform Jamaicans of the plans, policies, projects and day to day activities of the Government; to explain government's thinking on matters that affected the people and to help to generate an understanding of the country, its resources and possibilities for development. Mr. Manley recognized the need for a close and trusting relationship between the Government and People in the challenging times through which we were passing. The possibility of corrupting this straight-forward purpose was an inherent danger, somewhere down the road.

My father had been a Government Officer (civil servant) and both my grandfathers had served in public positions. I had a strong public service background. In my father's day partisan politics was not a factor. Allegiance was to the Monarch. Appointments had nothing to do with any political party. You couldn't be transferred or denied promotion on those grounds. Up to a certain level your ability, record of service and general demeanor were the determining factors. The great drawback was that top posts were reserved for British officials. Senior posts below them were usually filled by people who looked European, a hold-over from the days when it seemed necessary to align authority to a "Master Class."

Nevertheless, next to being an independent professional, my father were in favour of the civil service. A man of integrity, energy and ability had a fair chance and things were changing.

Neither my father nor I anticipated the kind of changes that were about to take place, as the country moved from the "security" of colonial status, to the rough, open-sea of parliamentary democracy.

In 1955, Norman Manley's government appointed Mr. A.E.T. Henry, a Jamaican, as Public Relations Officer of the newly set up Government Public Relations Office (GPRO). He took up duties the following year.

The GPRO occupied three of four rather dismal rooms at the back of Old Headquarters House at 79 Duke Street, Kingston, the home of the prestigious Colonial Secretariat. I shared a room with an authentic veteran named Claude Thompson, who instructed me in the writing of "Officialese", such as: *Further to your memorandum of even date, I forward herewith, etc, etc.*" It was like Jack Anderson at the Gleaner again, teaching me how to write "Journalese." Claude would fall asleep at his desk after lunch with an open newspaper masking his face. When he "bucked", the paper would dip and he would open his eyes.

The most outstanding event in those months took place Monday, November 11, 1957; the day of the inauguration of full internal self-government of Jamaica. The day before, Chief Minister, Norman Manley, broadcast a message over Radio Jamaica. He said:

"Tomorrow will see our own leaders take final charge of all our internal affairs. Tomorrow... is

Self-Government Day... Our Political conduct must be kept out of the gutters, where lies and slander and malice and intolerance reign. We must respect each other, because we are all Jamaicans and all part of humanity. We must remember that though all men are not born equal, all have an equal right to live and to enjoy the privileges and the opportunities of our countries.

"The greatest contribution (we) can make to the world is to prove that a society can be made where black and white and brown and yellow live together as men and women, in mutual harmony and shared respect."

Brave words, golden thoughts. If only we could make them a reality.

As an officer of the GPRO I was on duty at this unique ceremony, and I had to do a story for a booklet which the office planned to publish on the event. The day was declared a holiday. Thousands of people walked into Kingston's Parade Square. Lines of cars and packed buses rolled in. By half past eight, South Parade was thick with people, except for a roped-off area in front of Queen Victoria's statue (where Bustamante's statue now stands).

Just in front of the statue was a platform decorated with red, white and blue bunting. To one side was the zouave-uniformed Jamaica Military Band, with shining instruments. The crowd cheered as Chief Minister, the Hon. Norman Manley and Leader of the Opposition, Sir Alexander Bustamante, arrived. Bustamante had been knighted by Queen Elizabeth II in 1954, after he lost the General Elections.

Cheers rose again as Governor Sir Hugh Foot strode through Victoria Park (now renamed St. William Grant Park) and joined the leaders of church and state and other officials, on the platform. People lining the sidewalks cheered as a long column formed by the Army, Air Force, Cadets, St. John's Ambulance Brigade, Boys' Brigade, Boy Scouts, Girl Guides, Rovers, the Jamaica Youth Corps, the Worcestershire Regiment, the Jamaica Regiment and the Police, marched up the middle of the street towards South Parade.

The Governor took the salute as the ranks swung smartly past the platform. The Worcestershire Regiment, the Jamaica Regiment and the Police, coming up at the end of the column, formed three sides of the hollow square within the cleared area, with the platform making the fourth side. Just before nine o'clock, the Bugle Corps of the Worcestershire Regiment took up position in front of the platform, with their backs against it. A deep silence fell on the gathering and the whole Kingston Parade.

As the clock in the Memorial Tower of the Kingston Parish Church began to peal out the hour of nine, the buglers raised their instruments and sounded a dramatic fanfare. The last stroke on nine faded away. Governor Foot, standing before the microphone, began to read the proclamation giving full internal self-government to Jamaica, under a Council of Ministers. It was his last public, official act as Governor of Jamaica. When he finished reading, the crowd remained silent as if every person there was profoundly conscious of the giant leap the country was taking into the unknown.

In the awesome stillness, the voice of the Lord Bishop of Jamaica, the Rt. Rev Percival Gibson, rose clearly, sharply; praying for God's guidance. Still the silence gripped the crowd. It seemed that no one moved. The Worcestershire Regiment sloped arms and performed the Royal Salute, accompanied by the playing of the British National Anthem. Then the Governor turned and shook hands with dignitaries around him and descended the steps from the platform. Only then was the spell broken.

All at once the people came to life. They swarmed over the rope barriers and swirled about the platform, shouting for their leaders; laughing with spontaneous joy; feeling that they had at last won a victory in a long and hard fought war.

Three hours later, in the Council Chamber at Headquarters House, the Council of Ministers was sworn in by the Governor. The holiday mood persisted throughout the entire day. When night fell thousands thronged the George VI Memorial Park (now National Heroes Park) to witness a display of fireworks lasting nearly an hour.

Two thousand specially invited guests gathered on the "hallowed" lawns of the Myrtle Bank Hotel, for a cocktail party hosted by the Chief Minister. It was a merry scene; one of pride, hope and accomplishment. And so November 11, 1957, Self-Government Day, passed into history.

Putting Things Together

When I went to the GPRO, I reluctantly gave up the "10 o'clock World News Roundup" which I liked doing and for which I got a Talent Fee. The sponsors (Martin's Travel Service) wanted me to continue, but apparently A.E.T. couldn't get approval. I was now a civil servant. Extra work for pay was out. No more Talent Fees.

Fellow officers at GPRO included Hartley Neita (who was on a course at the Central Office of Information in London when I joined), Rose MacFarlane, Corina Meeks, Desmond Henry and Yvonne Mowatt. Corina was the very able head of our new Publications Sections, which soon began putting out a monthly magazine on the government's activities, among other things. A little later a photographic unit with a dark room facility was added and housed at the Film Unit. Top photographers Errol Harvey and Garth Morgan came on board.

Hartley thought A.E.T. Henry was a nice man, but I couldn't communicate with him, which was a bad thing since I was his assistant. One night, A.E.T. said, with a straight face:- *"Some people think I am short. But I am 5ft 71/2 inches tall. I am average height."* Everybody laughed, except A.E.T., he didn't even smile.

With some regret, I sold my old, green Austin A40 and bought a roomy, cream-coloured Morris Isis, with red upholstery. One day, A.E.T. asked me to call for him the next morning at about three, to drive him to an important function in the far west which was to be attended by the Chief Minister and I believe, the new Governor, Sir Kenneth Blackburn.

I was now renting the upstairs of Saxthorpe House on Constant Spring Road, having moved from my parents' home. Shortly after midnight I took an ice-cold bath in my chilly bath-room; dressed, ate something and picked up A.E.T. at his home.

In the dark of the early morning, the drive seemed eternal on the lonely roads. I concentrated on my driving, trying to stay awake. A.E.T. had bought a bottle of whiskey. He sipped from it gently, every now and then. We reached our destination early. When I sat in the grandstand to witness the event I fell asleep. Later, when we returned to Kingston, A.E.T. told me I was a good driver. The compliment made no impression on me.

Mr. W. Adolphe Roberts came to the GPRO one day. He was a much respected journalist, author and political activist; a sort of icon in the world of journalism. He had worked as a reporter at the Daily Gleaner as early as 1901, before going to the U.S.A. He founded the Progressive League of New York in 1936, which campaigned for the formation of a political party in Jamaica and for self-government. The League had a branch in Jamaica of which he had been president. Mr. Roberts showed me an old picture of Paul Bogle. I found that very exciting, because I had wrestled with the elusive image of Bogle while writing my Morant Bay Rebellion thesis at Howard. I was asked to keep the picture safe until it could be copied. The picture would one day serve as the official representation of Bogle on coins, bank notes, etc.

The GPRO soon moved from Headquarters House to 124 East Street. It was a dilapidated two-story structure. A small annex was built at the gate to house a reference library and distribution section, run by Lynwood Graham and Ken Williams. A.E.T. occupied a big room upstairs the main house with windows

and doors on every side. The rest of us were distributed throughout the building. The Film Unit was at the corner of Hanover
Street and North Street in another well-worn building. Broadcasting was at eleven Hagley Park Road, but was moved after a
while to the ground floor of the Town Planning Department at
5 South Odeon Avenue, Half Way Tree, the Jamaica Broadcasting
Corporation (JBC) would later be built.

The GPRO acquired a Mobile Cinema van with the Film Unit. In
a "raid" on the Jamaica Social Welfare Commission, we took over
cinema vans; most of them unserviceable. We gradually purchased
a few more until we had fourteen; one for each parish. In those
days, before television, the cinema vans were a great attraction in
deep rural areas, where there were no electricity and no cinemas.
The films came out of a collection of inherited material, including
ancient Mickey Mouse Cartoons, 5-year old newsreels, indifferent
short features, and documentaries from the British Information
Service and the USIS.

Disappointed audiences, driven crazy by stuff they had seen
three or four times, would heap abuse on the heads of the innocent
projectionists. As an antidote to the dreary environment at 124
East Street, and my inability to harmonize with my boss, I turned
to play-writing. I came up with a story about a plantation slave
who was in love with a slave girl who becomes the mistress of an
English bookkeeper and runs off into the hills. The play was
called "The Runaway," and was directed by Slade Hopkinson of
Guyana. Slade Hopkinson, like Derek Walcott and Bertram
Collins, was one of the "Whiz Kids" from the still-young University
of the West Indies. He worked with GPRO for a while. I enjoyed
the whole production, as did all the audiences. Harry Milner,
the newspaper critic, who came from a titled British family,
called the play a melodrama. But I told myself I did not leave as
many dead people on stage as Shakespeare did in Hamlet.

The Federation And JBC

The idea of a Federation of the West Indies had been in the air for a while. In 1932, politicians in the eastern Caribbean pressed for Guyana and Jamaica to join. In 1945 the Secretary of State for the Colonies invited the West Indian leaders to talk about a Federation. Bustamante, recently triumphant in the first General Elections in Jamaica, was not impressed. In 1947, he didn't attend a meeting of the Caribbean Labour Congress, called to take steps to set up a Federation based on internal self-government. He thought it didn't make sense to join a Federation of paupers. But after a conference in Montego Bay, he endorsed proposals for a Federation.

In 1956, the British Parliament passed an Act, setting up the Federation. It came into existence in January 1958. My sister's old professor, Dr. Eric Williams, had become Chief Minister of Trinidad and Tobago in 1956. He was a strong advocate of Federation. Norman Manley felt that Jamaica's political and economic development should be linked to the Federation, as it would be very difficult for us to "go it alone". But when elections were called in 1958 to elect a Federal Parliament, Eric Williams wasn't about to leave his newly-acquired seat of power in Trinidad and Tobago, to go into the federal government.

Norman Manley felt he dared not leave Jamaica, with Bustamante waiting defiantly on the sidelines to take back the reigns of power. Most people had expected Norman Manley to become the first Prime Minister of the Federal Parliament. A great deal of interest was lost when he said he wasn't running. In the Federal elections, Busta's Federal party won over Manley's. So it was a JLP dominated team which represented Jamaica in the Federal Parliament at Chagaramas in Trinidad.

In the mean time, the Jamaica Broadcasting Corporation (JBC) began to emerge. Government felt that the then foreign-owned RJR (popular and somewhat innovative as it was) could not provide the communications thrust for a self-governing Jamaica, that was steadily moving towards independence. So Government requested the Canadian Broadcasting Corporation (CBC) to send someone to do a report on broadcasting in Jamaica. The chairman of the CBC himself, Mr. Davidson Dunton, came down, studied the situation, and wrote a report.

Based on Dunton's report, the JBC was established, first by a Ministry Paper of January 31, 1958 and, almost a year later, by the JBC Law of December 19, 1958. During the months between, Mr. H.M. Smith of the CBC was brought in as a technical adviser. There was terrific excitement among people in broadcasting, journalism, the theatre and the arts, as the "Camelot" of broadcasting, which was being infused with the soaring hopes of the future, began to take shape. Norman Manley dedicated it to the life and growth of the new nation.

I was caught up in the excitement. I had thoughts of switching to the Corporation, if, by so doing, I could make more extensive use of my talent and experience, and help in the development of my country. But in October, 1958 shortly before the JBC Law confirmed the birth of the Corporation, Mr. Peer Aylen, Director of Radio and Visual Services of the United Nations, and a former executive of the CBC, took up duties as the first general manager of JBC.

Mr. Aylen looked very alien to me. He just didn't fit my image of the Chief Knight of the Jamaica Camelot. My enthusiasm began to waiver. I was to find that, where broadcasting was concerned, official Jamaica (being itself ignorant of the art) had little or no confidence in Jamaicans. It was tough enough for educated born-and-bred Jamaicans to understand what was happening in our country, and what kind of people we were. How on earth could a snow-bound Canadian, coming out of the United Nations New York Office, and without any experience of long-term living in Jamaica, be made the head of such a sensitive thing as our National Broadcasting station?

By January 1959, technical planning had reached the point where it was predicted that the station would go on the air around June. A nucleus of staff was housed at Marescaux Road. M.G. Robinson, who was with Government Broadcasting in the Town Planning Building at South Odeon (right next to the emerging JBC) was recruited to the Corporation's staff, as chief operator and supervisor of technical services. He worked along with H.M. Smith, the Canadian technical adviser, helping to install and test equipment, and recruit and train personnel. JBC would be going on the air with relatively untrained technical staff, to compete with RJR which had been in sole charge of the Jamaican radio scene for nearly ten years.

After a tremendous amount of hard and unremitting work, the technicians met their deadline. The station was officially launched on June 14, 1959. Reggie Carter, who had been making a name for himself as an actor, was the first announcer to go on the air. He later became programmes manager. Gordon Stewart (father of Gordon "Butch" Stewart) was the chief engineer. Hector Bernard (ex-Gleaner man) was appointed director of news.

Among those sending messages of congratulation were the Governor General of the West Indies Federation, Lord Hailes, and the Prime Minister of the Federation, the Barbadian, Sir Grantley Adams. That was the occasion when Chief Minister,

Norman Manley, made his heart-stirring speech, dedicating JBC to "the life and growth of the new nation".

Guyanese born Billy Pilgrim had been appointed director of music (I think) at the Corporation. He had knocked around with A.E.T. in London at the BBC, and he said to A.E.T.: *"Man, I thought you would be big in this thing (meaning JBC)."* A.E.T. murmured something about being on the Board; And indeed, a seat was reserved on the Board for whoever was head of the GPRO.

As I remember, Claude Thompson dropped out of the GPRO before we left Headquarters House. He had only been on a temporary assignment. I missed his humour, gentle tutelage and air of benevolent detachment. The stresses and strains that would develop with political change were still some distance in the future. We enjoyed a sort of camaraderie. It was a period of "innocence."

As the country approached independence it became necessary for the Government Broadcasting Service (the GBS) to change its way of operating. It controlled about 10½ hours of air-time weekly on RJR, 90% of this time was taken up by school's broadcasting and progammes for the British Council, the University of the West Indies, the churches, and various social service organizations. There were BBC and CBC transcriptions, occasional plays put on by an amateur drama group (mostly British expatriates), and a Jamaican extravaganza called "Poppyshow", produced by Ken Maxwell. Some approach was made to serious contemporary affairs through a brief programme or commentary. One of the regular commentators was an English man named E.H.J. King who taught at Jamaica College. It was a comfortable, conservative schedule, with the flavour of the passing colonial world.

As the GBS began altering course to accommodate the demands of self-government and approaching independence, I became peripherally involved, mostly with script-writing. In the midst of the transition, Ken Maxwell resigned, as government broad-casting officer. Because of my broadcasting experience and know-how, I was offered a lateral transfer from assistant public relations officer to broadcasting officer.

The offer came at the right time. I was becoming very uneasy as assistant to the government public relations officer; tagging along behind him to the airport, to King's House, to the Chief Minister's Office. More or less at his beck and call; living in his shadow. It wasn't my cup of tea. I was not a "boon companion." I accepted the lateral transfer with relief, and soared into the controls of the broadcasting space at a million miles an hour, at the controls of the GBS craft. John Hearne, a Jamaican author living in England, arrived to take up the post of assistant P.R.O. He had known A.E.T. in London and was a very good friend of Michael Manley. He had been a school mate of Michael Manley at Jamaica College.

The Government Broadcasting Service (GBS)

In my new sphere, my task was to reorganize The Government Broadcasting Service by devising programmes to reflect the plans, policies, projects and day-to-day activities of Government. Also, to keep radio listeners abreast of the challenges facing a newly self-governing country, and the role that responsible citizens had to play. In a "last ditch" effort to strengthen the Federation's image in Jamaica, the Service also attempted to get listeners thinking in regional terms, and to give them a clearer picture of the islands and territories which made up the Federation.

I was on my own. A.E.T. gave me a free hand. Routine supervision of my work wasn't possible. I had to get the facts right, at my own peril. Nobody in the Government Service had my know-how or hands-on experience. And (praise be to God) no "Foreign Expert" was brought down to fool around.

At the start, I had to do everything myself: write scripts, interview people, draw up a programme schedule, liaise with Government departments and agencies (largely with the help of our excellent Press Section), sometimes carry the fairly-heavy portable recorder on outside assignments and set it up and make the recording; devise names for programmes and choose themes, choose speakers or actors, read scripts, supervise editing, etc, etc. My newspaper and radio experience made it all possible.

Much of the government stuff was potentially "heavy." The challenge was to make the programmes interesting, palatable and thought-provoking. Ministers came on, quite willingly, and gave their talks. I remember lugging the portable recorder up to the Ministry of Agriculture early one morning to catch the Minister, Keeble Munn, coming down fresh from the cold Mavis Bank highlands.

Chief Minister, Norman Manley, came to the RJR studio one night to do a recording. When he was finished and I was escorting him to his car, he stopped and chatted with me. I was pleasantly surprised, because he could be so distant. He asked me about my work. He was so natural and genuinely curious, unassuming and kind. You'd never think he was the head of the country. But I was to feel the weight of his wrath some time later.

I produced documentaries, dramatizations, docu-drama, news programmes, features and magazine-type programmes. All kinds of people took part in the dramatizations including Charles Hyatt, one of Jamaica's foremost comics, and a young lawyer named Ian Ramsay, who briefly entered the political arena. Carol Reckord did wonderful monologues as Jack Naseberry, a fictional rural character, who gave pithy advice to farmers. Jack's programme had its own theme song:-

"Naseberry is a tree

that's plain for all to see..."

The dramatized programmes caught on like wild fire. One of the earliest was a series based on the Ministry of Health's Malaria Eradication Campaign. The hero was a Malaria Eradication Spray-man whose job was to go all about a community spraying in places where the malaria mosquito was likely to breed. His name was Raymond, and, not surprisingly, the series was called "Raymond the Spray-man." It had its own signature tune, which was based on the song "Around the World in Eighty Days."

"I'm Raymond the spray-man

I work all day,

And when I spray:

"Chip-chip-chip-chip" (a spraying sound)

Malaria goes away..."

In a few weeks, spray-men began to be greeted on the job by citizens, singing "I'm Raymond the Spray-man." Small boys ran after the spray-men shouting: *"Raymond the Spray-man, Raymond the Spray-man."* Before long, the Spray-men threatened to go on strike. They felt they were being disrespected. A deputation gathered in an office near the Kingston Public Hospital. I was summoned, and in anger was asked to take the series off air.

I assured the spray-men that no disrespect was meant. They referred to an episode where Raymond had attempted to spray a haunted house, and was almost forced to flee. I pleaded with them to have a sense of humor. Small boys would always be small boys, seeking for fun in everything. The warm response of people was a clear indication that the messages were getting across. No assault on their dignity was intended. They went back to work. The campaign was a great success.

Another very popular series was "Corporal Clooney," based on a Government Road Safety Campaign. The Corporal was a dedicated, policeman with a gruff voice, and an authoritative presence. He was well liked by the people among whom he worked.

He gave firm advice on the proper ways to use the roads. Corporal Clooney was played by Henri Hendricks, the younger brother of RJR's Mickey Hendricks. The chief nuisance in the Corporal's community was an amusing fellow name Sputnik (which was the name given to the current space Satellite of the Soviet Union). Sputnik was played by the very popular comedian, Charles Hyatt.

Sometime during this period, Elaine Perkins (wife of Wilmot "Motty" Perkins) came to see me about script-writing. I found out later that her maiden name was Barton and that she was the granddaughter of old Mr. Barton (Father B), who had been a respected veteran of the Gleaner Editorial Department while I was there.

I gave her a test assignment, something to do with the Ministry of Health. The script she wrote was very good, and she started with us soon after. It was a relief to find someone who could write so well. It took a big load off me. Elaine had a gift for writing natural-sounding dialogue, which was not patronizing. She could create life-like characters and inject refreshing humor, which made it easy for listeners to receive serious messages.

Meanwhile JBC came on stream, headed by Canadian Peter Aylen. The Corporation took over the non-government programmes (by the churches, the university, the British Council, etc.) which had used up alot of government broadcasting time. Schools Broadcasting was taken over by the Ministry of Education, and the GBS was now free to get on with its information/public service agenda.

Peter Aylen, faced with formidable competition from the entrenched RJR, and wanting to do something different, was uncertain how to programme the vital early morning segment. Aylen asked me what I thought about putting someone like Charles Hyatt on the morning shift, with a sort of semi-dialect grass-roots approach. I don't remember what I told him, but the experiment he had in mind didn't work. It would probably have been all right for a feature, but not for morning-time continuity.

Sometime during that first year, a listeners' survey was done. It had at least one unexpected result. I was now recording GBS programmes at the JBC. One day I was on my way to the studio when I encountered Aylen. He said: *"The survey shows that your programmes are just about the most popular on the station."* I was totally surprised. I wasn't even thinking of Government programmes in competition with anything. I regarded them as separate and apart. I gave silent thanks to "Raymond the Sprayman", "Corporal Clooney", "Sputnik" and all the rest.

Aylen left in 1960, after about a year. He had only been "on loan" from the United Nations. He was succeeded by Captain William Strange, another Canadian, who had served in his country's navy. Jamaicans, still nursing a giant-size inferiority complex where broadcasting was concerned, did not as yet dare to appoint a Jamaican to the top post. Reggie Carter, with "tongue in cheek," referred to Bill Strange as "the strange Captain." Strange had a burly physique, and was very much the ex-serviceman. He set about making changes, but he didn't understand the political culture that was starting to develop and began to rub some people the wrong way.

Looking on from the outside, it seemed to me that the national station was being led by a team of non-Jamaicans; starting with the general manager on top, flanked by "Whizz-kids" such as Lloyd Brydon (American), Esse Ljungh (Canadian), Robin Midgley (British), Bill Pilgrim (Guyanese), and one or two others whose names I can't remember. Somewhat below them were other "lights," such as Carlos Malcolm from Panama, Kerry Adams from the U.K. (she was part West Indian), Howard Clarke from Canada, and Pat Barton from the U.S., Rita Coore, though married to David Coore (Jamaican lawyer and politician) was from Trinidad. They all gave a decidedly international quality to the fledgling national station. But despite everything, durable, foreign-owned RJR continued to dominate the broadcasting scene.

GBS got a chance to enhance its reputation when Gordon House was opened as the new home for the Government. The Legislature had been meeting regularly at Headquarters House, 79 Duke Street, since the capital was removed from Spanish Town to Kingston in 1872. It had obviously out grown that historic building, so the new Legislature building was constructed just north of Headquarters House. It was named after George William Gordon. He was a member of the old House of Assembly, who had been accused of instigating the Morant Bay Rebellion and was executed in 1865.

I decided that GSB should do a dramatized programme on Gordon's life, to mark the opening of the new Legislature. Elaine Perkins wrote a very good script which I produced. Reggie Carter did an excellent job as George William Gordon. We all felt elated that we had been able to make such a first-rate contribution to mark the occasion.

On the day Gordon House was officially opened (October 26, 1960) I was in Headquarters House for the ceremony of transition "from the Old to the New." Our Film Unit was outside filming Premier Norman Manley inspecting the Guard of Honour. I remember watching Bustamante coming out of the Opposition Room at Headquarters House at the head of his team, walking towards the big chamber where the Legislature met. He came out immaculately dressed, walking easy, in his fearless manner and with his challenging eyes. He dominated the scene. I was hardly aware of the others behind him. He was talking as he came. I was standing near the doorway to the big chamber. He looked hard at me as he passed close by, challenging me with his eyes. I stood straight up. I don't know if he recognized me from our meeting in the house at Mocho.

Anybody who was even the least bit aware and honest, would have to admit that Jamaica was becoming a very difficult place to understand. On the one hand intellectuals and political activists were talking scathingly about wicked colonialism. On the other hand ordinary people were tremendously uplifted and excited by visits from royalty and Winston Churchill. Thousands of poor Jamaicans were streaming to Britain as a land of opportunity where they could start a new life; many came from deep rural areas, with tropical clothing on their backs, to face their first cold winter.

The British Government was actively encouraging migration. They needed workers to fill thousands of jobs in their cities. From the end of World War II, in 1945, migration to Britain had started; a mere trickle at first, but growing rapidly. Over 17,000 Jamaicans went in 1956. In 1957, 13,087 left; followed by 9,992 in 1958, and 12,796 in 1959. In 1960, the year Gordon House was opened, 32,060 migrated. In 1961, the figure exceeded 39,000. Poor, ambitious Jamaicans were trying to tell the country something which many did not stop to hear or understand. Forty years later, the children and grandchildren of these migrants would be helping to transform Britain, which, with all its insularity and fear of outsiders, had given them opportunities for education and training which they couldn't get at home, and which would fit many to perform creditably at every level. Britain seemed more willing to be transformed than the United States.

Side by side, with the migration to Britain, thousands were flocking to the United States, as their parents and grandparents had turned to Cuba, Costa Rica and Panama in earlier times. With all the talk of nationalism here, there was still a deep self-doubt and dependence on the thinking of other people. On top of all that was the division of opinion over whether to go into independence as part of the Federation, or go in on our own.

Rising through the clouds of indecision, confusion, conflict and neglect was the Rastafarian Movement. Norman Manley called on us to feel that our life and destiny were irrevocably bound up with the life and destiny of the country. The Rastas, however, dismissed Jamaica as Babylon. Their cry was "Africa."

The Wreck Of The Federation

Many Jamaicans didn't know what to make of the Caribbean leaders. There was a small, dapper Eric Williams, looking enormously serious and intellectual behind his dark glasses; Grantley Adams of Barbados, a tall stoop-shouldered, lumbering man with a heavy-accent and a commanding look; Vere Bird of Antigua, 6 feet 4, seeming too astute and unshakeable; Robert Bradshaw with his luxuriant moustache, a man who sometimes dressed in a kind of costume with knee breeches; Eric Gairy, a charismatic, indisciplined and troublesome man from Grenada; William Bramble of Montserrat, a sturdy man of the people; etc. The federal capital was all the way down at Chagaramas in Trinidad. Norman Manley wasn't going down there. Who would rule us long-distance from that place? We wanted to rule our selves.

Matters grew worse when Sir Grantley Adams, Prime Minister of the Federation, hinted that the Federal Government would have power over national governments. He said something about "retrospective taxation" that mystified most people. It was taxation that could be applied "backwards," apparently taking effect from some date in the past. People weren't sure what he meant but it sounded menacing.

Adam's remark roused Bustamante. He demanded that if Jamaica was to remain in the Federation, the Federal Government should have no right to impose any kind of taxation on the country, without our consent. Busta went on to declare that representation in the Federal House should be based on population (Jamaica had the largest population and would therefore have the most seats.) He further insisted that no Customs Union should be set up which would hurt the island's trade. Once again Busta seemed to be emerging as the people's champion, in the face of apparent threats to their well-being and future.

Norman Manley, the champion of Federation, was caught at a disadvantage. The federal cause was being discredited in the eyes of many Jamaicans, and the 1959 General Elections were coming up. Manley was forced to agree with Bustamante. But he still had enough support to win the 1959 General Elections of July 28; PNP 29 seats, JLP 16. The Council of Ministers had been replaced by a Cabinet headed by a Premier just before the elections. So when Norman Manley once more took his place at the helm, it was as Premier, rather than as Chief Minister.

Sir Grantley Adams opened his mouth again and made things even worse for Norman Manley. He boasted that Barbadians were a superior people, compared to Jamaicans and Trinidadians. Jamaica with its high rate of illiteracy, and Trinidad with its carnival mentality, was definitely trailing behind. Eric Williams jumped in next, accusing the Federal Government of being a stooge for the Colonial office. Williams wanted a strong Federation, which would control the economic development of the whole region. With the capital situated in his own country, maybe he saw himself as the coming Caesar of the West Indies.

Bustamante, taking advantage of every favourable shift in the wind, announced that his party would not contest the up-coming Federal Elections. To crown that decision his party declared that it was opposed to Jamaica remaining in the Federation. Cornered by these developments, Norman Manley announced that a referendum would be called to settle the issue.

It was one thing coming together to create a University of the West Indies, or to form a West Indies cricket team; but a Federation was a different thing; a very serious business. It was government, and government meant having power over people's lives. In the midst of the growing uncertainty, the Government Broadcasting Service explored the potential benefits of federation. We examined several federations, some set up before the birth of Christ. We also looked at federation in British Commonwealth countries, such as Australia and Canada. One day Norman Manley was speaking to a group at his home (Drumblair) about the Canadian Federation. He was talking about the English Governor who had recommended the union of the provinces of Upper and Lower Canada. He paused in mid-sentence, groping for the name of the Governor, I blurted out: *"Lord Durham."* He turned and looked at me in astonishment. I had to thank the History Department at Howard for that one. Apart from examining federations, we starred in a dramatic series with characters from various West Indian islands. A little romance was thrown in, after all, there were many examples of Caribbean men and women who had married Jamaicans and were living in Jamaica. But events were soon to overtake all our efforts. The day of decision arrived on September 19, 1961, when the referendum promised by Norman Manley was held. Should Jamaica remain in the Federation, or should we drop out? 256, 261 people voted for the country to drop out. 217,319 voted for it to remain. The majority had spoken. We dropped out. Soon after that the Federation collapsed. Jamaica asked for Independence. Britain agreed to give it to us on August 6, 1962. In about the 1930s a former Governor of Jamaica, Lord Olivier, wrote a book called "Jamaica, the Blessed Island." In it he wrote that some "imperfectly educated" persons say that Jamaica must obviously become a federal unit in the Government of a West Indian Dominion. But Olivier said:

"It does not appear to Jamaicans that their community could in any way gain by (federation), either in material advantage or in prestige and consideration. (They) are also aware that Jamaica lies a thousand miles distant from the other British Antilles, with no likelihood of more than fort-nightly communications. (They) will never consent to having the domicile of their Government outside the island, and in so essentially different a political and social atmosphere as that of Barbados or Trinidad."

It is easier now to get from Jamaica to the "other British Antilles" than it was at the time Lord Olivier wrote this. But apart from that, one wonders if he was wrong in his judgment.

Some years after the collapse of the Federation, when Forbes Burnham of Guyana and Eric Gairey of Grenada, were riding high; and stubborn Eric Williams of Trinidad and Tobago seemed immovable, an acquaintance suggested to me that it was the providence of God that had taken us out of the Federation. Otherwise there would have been bloodshed. Someone like Gairey or Burnham or Bishop would have seized hold of it, and tried to impose a dictatorship. We would have had to fight our way out.

All who had pushed hard for federation seemed deflated. A show-down hung over the Government Public Relations Office. But something had to be done. Independence was just around the corner. Matters were made more urgent by Norman Manley's decision to call General Elections three years earlier than he had to. It was a tough decision but he felt that the results of the referendum demanded that he call elections, so the people could decide whether they wanted his party or Busta's to lead the country into Independence. The collapse of the federal movement had knocked him flat; made him sick. And that was an alarming thing, for he was a man with a terribly strong will.

For my part I thought I had better start doing something on the Government Broadcasting Service (GBS) about Independence. A.E.T. Henry was different. He too seemed crushed, as if he sensed that some other disaster was about to happen, which he could do nothing to prevent. He was working for the government on contract. If the government fell, his position would be precarious.

Norman Manley's acute awareness of his tremendous, personal efforts to bring about self-government and independence, as opposed to Bustamante's late conversion was forcibly brought home to me when I did a docu-drama on Jamaica's history. Mr. Manley felt that, at the end of the programme, the impression was given that both he and Bustamante had worked with equal zest for self-government and independence. He exploded; "hit the roof," "blew his top." How could anybody make such a colossal error. That's when I felt the weight of his wrath, though it was at long-distance and not face-to-face.

There were a couple of other pitfalls ahead, though much less horrendous. I started some independence programmes. One series was called: "Citizens of a New Jamaica." The whole idea was to stir up thought about a short list of eminent persons to talk about independence. I hoped to get something positive that would be helpful.

I briefed the people on my list of what we wanted to achieve. Among the speakers was the much-respected economist, Sir Arthur Lewis, who was born in St. Lucia. When I recorded his speech I was shocked. He was saying, in effect, that he thought Jamaica had made a mistake in deciding to go into Independence on its own. In my state of hot-headedness I felt he should not have accepted my invitation to speak if he was going to discourage us. I edited the tape to tone down some of the negatives. When he heard the broadcast he couldn't believe his ears. He didn't "hit the roof," as Norman Manley had done, but I am told he turned to someone and said: *"who is this Mr. Robinson?"* I was also summoned by Mr. Hugh Shearer over some editing that had been done to a talk he had recorded. I don't think I did the editing, but I was the responsible officer. Mr. Shearer was then a top man in the Bustamante Industrial Trade Union (the BITU). He sternly rebuked me and I apologized. Without doubt I was rapidly learning a lot from these incidents. Mr. Shearer would one day become Prime Minister of Jamaica.

Another time I was going down the stairs at JBC after having done a recording. A slender, very youthful-looking man was standing at the desk of the receptionist. He turned and gave me a half smile and said good afternoon. I recognized him as the person who had recently made a very provocative speech about "the haves and have-nots". Overnight his name was on the lips of almost everyone. It was Edward Seaga, the young, new face in Bustamante's JLP. He too would one day become Prime Minister of Jamaica.

Political Change

Norman Manley had made a tremendous effort to win a yes vote for the Federation in the referendum; but support had been falling away, even inside his own party. His personal vision for the future of Jamaica was being destroyed before his eyes. Nevertheless, there was hope. He might win the General Elections, called for April 10, 1962. But Bustamante and his party swept to power, winning 26 seats to the PNP's 19. If the referendum had stunned Norman Manley, the loss of the General Elections was a cruel blow, delivered while he was still down. He had laboured long and hard for Independence. Now he had to stand by and watch while his arch rival, Bustamante, led the nation up to that pinnacle of statehood. Manley's obvious depression was reflected in many who revered him.

Immediately after the elections, a very senior member of the GPRO approached me, with a grave countenance. *"Some of us will be resigning,"* he said, *"as we are not prepared to work with the new Government. What about you?"*

His words sounded like a threat; as if there would be serious consequences if I didn't fall in line. I was flabbergasted for a moment. I thought to myself: *"who the hell does this cat think he is?"* I had come out of the maw of Jim Crow, hoping to help to build something of dignity and worth in my own country. I leap-frogged from one job to another and finally found something I could really get my teeth into; something that seemed to hold out a real opportunity. And here was this 'cat' trying to intimidate me; trying to take over my mind. Where did he expect me to go? Having received my negative answer, 'the cat' went away, looking more sourly than when he arrived. Not long after, we received a summons from the new Minister, the Hon. Eward Seaga, under whose portfolio the GPRO now fell. Except for "the cat", who had disappeared, A.E.T. and his senior officers (including myself) were ushered into the Minister's Office on the appointed day. We sat around a table, which formed the leg of a T with his desk. This time I detected no smile. He was serious. There were no frivolous preliminaries. It was down to business at once. *"What have you done to help prepare the country for Independence?"* There was dead silence. We were all waiting on A.E.T. After a moment or two I opened a file I had brought which contained my "stuff." *"Well"*, I said, *"I've been doing a radio series on Independence."* I took out several scripts and gave them to him. He glanced through them rapidly and said: *"Yes,"* as if in acknowledgement of my efforts, *"but this is not enough."* He then gave us a general idea of what he expected us to do. It was obvious he wasn't going to tolerate any foot-dragging organization. A.E.T. left the GPRO not long after, and as the senior "surviving" officer, I was appointed to act as the government public relations officer. Doom-sayers immediately appeared, to fill me with gloom: *"That's not the kind of job for you,"* *"You won't be able to stand up to them."* *"They'll eat you (nyam you) raw."*

During those early days, a big question mark hung over the GPRO. Had it become the creature of the Government which had set it up? Would it now (inevitably) have to become the creature of the new Government? Or would it be able to function, within accepted guidelines, like any other Government department? For although A.E.T. had been a "contract officer," the rest of us were civil servants.

The popular concept of a Public Relations Organization was

one whose job was to white-wash, and manipulate the minds of people for selfish or sinister reasons. Some senior officials saw the GPRO as a type of "entertainment." A plaything.

In a sense we were breaking new ground. We had to win respect. But something had to be done to change that name: "Government Public Relations Officer." It was to be established whether the head of the organization could be a qualified career civil servant, or whether it must be headed by a contract officer, chosen for loyalty to an incumbent Government, and expected to resign when the Government changed. I hadn't even begun to think seriously of these matters, in spite of A.E.T.'s fate. I continued to have an "idealistic" vision. My head was just full of work. The country was on the threshold of Independence: People needed to know what was going on, and we were privileged to help them find out. Up to about the time of the General Elections we enjoyed a pretty good camaraderie at GPRO. But when we passed through the fire of political change, I had a feeling that "the age of innocence" was over. As the acting "Boss", subject to be dethroned at any time for the slenderest of reasons I began to feel very isolated.

While things were in limbo, Hartley Neita and I went to see Prime Minister Bustamante, to try to make some kind of contract. Busta came out of his inner sanctum, very smartly dressed and looking relaxed and cheerful. He sat down and, in a genial manner, asked us what we wanted. I said we just wanted to introduce ourselves and get an idea of how to proceed with our work, as far as he was concerned. I think that's more or less what I said. Busta sat back in his chair and burst out laughing. *"I don't know if you fellows are smart enough,"* he said; and sort of left us hanging in the air. My failure to get through to Busta got me into trouble later on. When I was transferred to the post of broad-casting officer, I had moved into a room on the ground floor where I kept my tapes, batteries and recording equipment. It was private, away from the upstairs clutter, and I liked it. As acting public relations officer, I refused to move into A.E.T.'s old office upstairs, with its doors and windows on every side, and the adjacent rooms chock-full of staff and desks. So I stayed right where I was. Unfortunately, I forgot to transfer the private phone to my office downstairs. Our Minister had the straight-line number. He called me. By the time I ran up to the phone he had been waiting a little, and that annoyed him. I had the straight line moved down in the shortest possible time.

With the approach of Independence Day (August 6, 1962) the GPRO's Film Unit, under Martin Rennalls, went into action; covering the arrival of Princess Margaret (she was deputizing for the Queen) and activities in key areas in various parts of the island. Including the grand ceremony at the new stadium at midnight, with the British Union Jack coming down, and the new Jamaican black, green and gold flag going up.

The film was called "A Nation is Born," and it touched the heart. It has proved to be a most important historical record, which will probably be of inestimable value for as long as there is a Jamaican Nation. Among the things captured by the film was Prime Minister Bustamante dancing awkwardly with Princess Margaret at the Grand Ball. Bustamante had little regard for the "fussiness" of protocol. He seemed incapable of "kow-towing" or of placing anyone on a pedestal. While dancing with Princess Margaret it is alleged that he enquired about Her Majesty the Queen by asking:-

"And how is your sister?"

U.S Vice President (and future President) Lyndon Johnson had come to the Independence celebrations as his country's representative. He was standing with Bustamante on a platform at South Parade, watching the troops march past to music played by the band of the U.S. Aircraft Carrier, Lake Champlain, on which he had arrived. Impressed by the large crowd, he is alleged to have said to Bustamante: *"What is the population of Kingston, Mr. Prime Minister?"* But Busta was concentrating intently on the scene and simply said: *"Eh!"* Mr. Johnson tried again. *"What's the population of Kingston?" "Eh,"* again from the inattentive Busta, busy watching the parade. Mr. Johnson once more:-*"How many people are here in Kingston?"* To which Bustamante is alleged to have replied:- *"Plenty, plenty."*

It was the sort of story that Bustamante increasingly and inevitably seemed to attract to himself. Because he was such an unusual man, he generated the kind of stuff that was made for mystery, legend and folklore.

A thing like an Information Service wasn't part of Bustamante's personal universe. He was his own public relations and information officer. He was a man most at home with a crowd in the open, or among poor folk in the interior of a shop, gathered over a modest meal. It was no accident that I had been unable to get through to him when I visited his office in his early days as Prime Minister. But it resulted in a rather uncomfortable experience. One day he wanted a cameraman to cover some events. So he asked somebody (perhaps his secretary) to phone the Film Unit and tell them to send up a cameraman. No one went. Bustamante erupted like a volcano and apparently went to the Minister and raised hell. The Minister phoned me at once and blamed me for the cameraman's absence. If I couldn't do the job, he said, then maybe he ought to find somebody else who could. I told him, as calmly as I was able, that I didn't know what he was talking about. I had received no request for a cameraman. I asked him if he could please ensure that the next time the Prime Minister, or any of his ministers, had a request for the services of any section of the GPRO, that the request be made to me. Thankfully the Prime Minister immediately got the point. It had been a gut-wrenching experience.

Camelot And JIS

JBC, like the GPRO, was having to adjust to the changed political scene. But JBC wasn't rooted in the civil service like the GPRO was, so it didn't weather the storm of change as well. When the Corporation was in the planning stage, a decision had to be made about whether it should be funded from the public, (like the BBC), or partly commercial and partly from the public (the state) like the Canadian Broadcasting Corporation (CBC). The latter model was chosen. JBC should try to earn revenue from commercials and the sponsoring of programmes. But, if there was a shortfall, there was an unwritten agreement that the government would make up the difference. That was Norman Manley's personal commitment to the development of a national station. And, of course, the land and the plant of the Corporation belonged to the government. Any talk of an independent, JBC was therefore wishful thinking. But nobody really stopped to consider that at the time. RJR down at 32 Lyndhurst Road, held on to its lead and kept on attracting the major share of commercial revenue. But in the early days no one was really worried. As long as Norman Manley was here, everything would be alright. With the draining away of the British presence, it seemed to many aspiring, educated Jamaicans that Norman Manley was the ideal person to establish a new leadership class, rooted in Jamaica. In the first intoxicating flowering of self-government, he gathered around him a group of very able public servants, who had come out of the excellent Jamaican Colonial Civil Service. Thousands of bright young civil servants received special training. Hundreds were trained in Britain.

Norman Manley appeared like a sort of King Arthur, gathering the best Knights for his Round Table, to build a Camelot in Jamaica. His home at Drumblair became a kind of court, a gathering place for the beautiful and talented; the "bright lights."

The setting up of JBC was accompanied by the same high hopes: a focal point for the intellectuals and the artistic. It didn't seem to occur to anyone that with the heavy reliance on government assistance, there would be an obligation not to offend the government, and even perhaps to support it. The head of Government was, after all, the father of the Corporation. When Captain William Strange left the Corporation in 1961, the Board appeared to be ready to take the chance of appointing a Jamaican to the post of general manager, which was then regarded as a very high and prestigious position. Mickey Hendricks, Sales Manager of RJR, was appointed to the post. He brought a bunch of RJR people with him, including Kay Dupee as administrative assistant, Merrick Needham as programme manager and Tino Barovier as supervisor of sales and programme administration. The JBC seemed to have taken on a new life, and appeared to give RJR some powerful competition. Then N.W. Manley lost the General Elections of 1962, and Camelot seemed to shudder. The unwritten agreement that government would take care of any shortfalls experienced by the Corporation came under fire. There was a feeling that JBC must learn to run itself like a business, and pay its way, even if some of the 'worthy' Public Service Programmes had to be replaced by "popular" stuff, which could bring in some money and cost less to produce. It was the beginning of a period of increasing grief for the Corporation, marked by escalating internal strife and growing doubts about its impartiality. As acting head of the GPRO I found myself on the new Board of the JBC.

At about this time, with the Minister's approval, I began to grope for a new name for the GPRO. At first I thought of "Government Information Service." But the word "Government" still felt wrong. The word "Jamaica" entered my head and sounded right.

Very shortly after, Mickey Hendricks phoned to suggest that the GPRO be changed to "The Jamaica Information Service" (JIS). Had Mickey been reading my mind? The Minister thought it was a splendid idea.

The early Independence years of the 1960s were tremendously busy and exciting. Shortly after Independence, Jamaica became a member of the United Nations. Our first U.N. Representative was none other than Edgerton Rudolph Richardson, former financial secretary.

Our first "native" Governor General, Sir Clifford Campbell, was knighted by the Queen and installed at King's House, once the residence of Colonial Governors. The Prime Minister, Sir Alexander Bustamante, was made a member of the Privy Council of England. There was a joyful feeling of expectancy; much like a Christmas morning, when you got eagerly awake to see what presents Santa Clause had brought. Mr. Donald Sangster, Minister of Finance, was made Deputy Prime Minister, and a Jamaican girl, Carol Joan Crawford, won the Miss World Contest (1963), the first Jamaican girl to win the title.

The next year (1964), JIS put out a booklet as part of the three hundred years of parliamentary government in Jamaica. Deputy Prime Minister Sangster was keen to establish a conscious link with the old Colonial Legislature and the Crown Colony period (following the Morant Bay Rebellion) as "a decisive reversal of two hundred years since the inception of a measure of representative government." The booklet also helped to highlight the presentation of "the gift of a Speaker's Chair by the Parliament of Great Britain to the Parliament of Jamaica." That same year (1964), Marcus Garvey was made our first National Hero. He had died in England in 1940 and had been buried there. His remains were disinterred, brought to Jamaica and buried with ceremony at the George VI Memorial Park (now National Heroes Park) in November. The JIS Film Unit did a valuable film on the arrival of Garvey's remains, the procession through the streets, and the burial in the park. Garvey's elevation to National Hero sent a message to the Jamaican people, especially to the more than 90 percent who were of African descent. They only got a part of it, which was that in Jamaica, colour could no longer be tolerated as a barrier against them.

Our Minister played a big part in bringing back Garvey's remains. I drafted a fact sheet about Garvey which was found to be too hard-hitting. Bitter feelings were needlessly aroused. I had to tone it down considerably.

Shortly after Bustamante was made Prime Minister in 1962, he married Gladys Longbridge, his faithful private secretary of many years. She had stood by him through thick and thin, without flinching. At the age of seventy-eight Bustamante appeared to take a new and more benevolent lease on life. He seemed as indestructible as Jupiter on Mount Olympus. But in 1964, he fell ill, and Deputy Prime Minister, Donald Sangster, was appointed to act as Prime Minister. Bustamante had seemed almost indifferent to the communications media. Face-to-face with a crowd he was at home. But with just a microphone to talk to he appeared to be out of his element. Mr. Sangster however, had definite expectations as far as JIS was concerned. The top post was still called Government Public Relations Officer. As far as Mr. Sangster was concerned that meant someone who was almost a member of his personal staff. He phoned and asked why I wasn't at his office every morning. I explained that I had a highly-visible and complex organization to run, but I could always be reached if he needed me. In addition, a senior press officer had been assigned exclusively to his office. I don't think he was entirely satisfied with my reply. Would he have me removed from my position? That wouldn't be difficult, for I was only acting, and therefore subject to removal at any time.

Some pressure came from senior civil servants in our ministry. But apart from keeping an eye on expenditure, they usually left us alone, being ignorant of almost every aspect of our creative work. Nevertheless, a senior official, who shall remain nameless, summoned me to his office one day, and asked that I bring relevant files. He was a man I knew well. I had enjoyed animated discussions with him about the merits and achievements of old-times strong men like Louis Cyr and the Saxon brothers. Now he wore an arrogant mask of authority, and addressed me in a commanding voice.

I thought he must be losing his mind, but for old-times sake, I tried not to show my concern. However, I lost my cool when he suggested regular meetings at which I would report to him. The guy was obviously looking for something to do. I berated him for his hostile manner and told him I didn't think regular meetings were necessary, or could work. I more or less suggested that he leave me alone to get on with my job. If I needed help I would ask for it. I was again amazed at my capacity for recklessness.

Television

In August, 1962, there was an exciting experiment during Independence Week. The new government gave permission for Philips Electrical Industries Ltd. of Holland, and the Gleaner Company Ltd., to set up a Closed Circuit TV system through which people in Kingston could see the ceremonial Opening of Parliament by Princess Margaret, including the handing over of the "Instruments of Independence" to Prime Minister Bustamante.

A temporary studio, with equipment flown in from Holland, was set up in the old Council Chamber at Headquarters House on Duke Street. Television receiving sets were put up at Victoria Park (now St. William Grant Park), Coke Hall and Gordon House. Perry Henzel (of Vista Productions, who was to make the film "The Harder They Come") was in charge of the nightly show. It featured news, commentaries, and I remember RJR's Charlie Babcock and "Brim" Brimble being on the shows. From 8 pm to 10 pm each night, thousands of people gathered at the receiving sets to watch Jamaica's "first venture into TV." On the day of the Opening of Parliament, thousands who couldn't possibly witness the historic ceremony inside Gordon House, were able to see it on the sets.

With that brief taste of the magic of television, many were now eager for the real thing. Government hinted it would come soon, and there was much speculation about who would get the licence.

Mickey Hendricks, first Jamaican general manager of the Jamaica Broadcasting Corporation (JBC) felt he held a solidly strong position, and was in a confident, high-striding mood. At the fifth

Commonwealth Broadcasting Conference in Canada, he told a gathering of colleagues that JBC "was free to criticize the Government and battle with (it) if need be, on matters of principle." Appointed the year before the elections, he appeared to be in good standing with the new Board selected by the new JLP Government.

Its new chairman, K.H. Ivan Levy, got together a consortium of overseas interests that was prepared to make a loan, at reasonable rates, to set up and run a television station. It was also willing to provide managing agency service and technical expertise.

The consortium was made up of Thompson Television International, the National Broadcasting Company of America (NBC), Grenada Television of Great Britain, and Television International Enterprises of London. Experts from Scottish Television were also thrown in. Backed by the Consortium, JBC applied for an exclusive licence to operate television services. The proposal was submitted to Parliament by the Hon. Edward Seaga, Minister of Development and Welfare, under whose portfolio broadcasting fell. Unanimous approval was given and everyone was excited.

The "ultimate magic" was finally arriving. But some felt that television was an expensive luxury for which Jamaica was not ready. Radio, after two decades in Jamaica, had still not been fully exploited. Now we were about to be enslaved by a gadget that has been called everything from the "Idiot's Lantern, to the One-eyed Monster, to the new opiate of the people (Spotlight Magazine)." But nothing could hold back the rush to enter the "New Age," in which the whole world could see itself, and where one could witness events unfolding in places that one would probably never visit. JBC was granted the franchise to operate a television service in November 1962, almost coinciding with Jamaica's entry into the new age of political independence. Prime Minister Sir Alexander Bustamante, now seventy-eight, wielded the pickaxe which broke ground for the television studio buildings at 5 South Odeon Avenue, on January 31, 1963.

The opening date was set for August, which left only a few months for the operation to be completed. Overseas experts descended on JBC, and with the Corporation's staff, worked around the clock at a feverish pace. The chief engineer was Mike Hately an Englishman. He was ably supported by Essex born Laurie Stewart, senior maintenance engineer for television. Test transmissions were carried out from Studio Three in the Radio building in June. The few Jamaicans with television sets saw a JBC employee named Joyce Fisher on the screens, the first person to appear on Jamaican TV, so to speak. JBC had to provide Government with at least half an hour daily of television time for programmes produced by JIS. We had to find staff and train them without delay. We got our quota of foreign experts. I called them "the two Johns." John Furness of the BBC (Nicked-name "the Fury Furnace" by his BBC colleagues), and John Irving. Furness was mostly concerned with programmes production and Irving was primarily with film. As could have been predicted, a lunatic idea for success was put forward by a senior civil servant bureaucrat. All we had to do was get some beauty queens and put them on camera. We were also advised to stock-pile as many programmes on film as we could, against the opening day. Nobody realized what a voracious appetite Television had, and how rapidly it consumed material. We were conditioned by a culture in which a film ran for several nights in turn. Stock-piling was definitely not the answer, not when you were committed to pro-ducing a progamme every day.

Initially JIS-TV was situated on the ground floor of the old Town Planning building on the JBC compound. Equipment for schools broadcasting, donated by the United States Government, was stored on the second floor of the building. We needed that second floor to take care of the rapidly expanding JIS-TV, and we asked the Ministry of Education to find somewhere else to store the equipment. They agreed but did nothing. Our expansion deadline was approaching. We reminded them of their promise; but bureaucratic inertia was at work, and nothing happened. Our Minister phoned to find out how things were going, and when I told him about the stalemate, he said: *"Move them out."* That was all. The next day was a Saturday, if I remember correctly. I got a few men and moved all the U.S. donated equipment to a couple of empty rooms on the ground floor, without asking anybody's permission. When they turned up on Monday morning, they were astonished. The resident U.S official (I think he was USAID) was livid. He almost tore out his hair. The affair nearly caused a minor international incident. When the irate official saw our office attendant (Rennel Carr) about to dust the equipment he shouted: "Don't touch that!" Rennel spun around and demanded that he not speak to her in that manner. But things cooled down in no time. John (Fury) Furness started classes with the tiny JIS-TV staff, including myself, Audrey Chong, Ken Jones, Joyce Constable and one or two others. We learned the TV scriptwriting format and got help from JBC's carpenter and props-man in making and erecting flats and sets of all kinds. The lighting engineer introduced us to the techniques of lighting. John Irving in the mean time was helping to transform the Film Unit into a fast-shooting outfit capable of meeting the TV demand. We established a Processing and Printing laboratory for 16 and 35mm films, and full sound-mixing and dubbing facilities. Video-tape was not yet on the scene.

When the JBC Television studio was just about ready, we learned to use it and give instructions to the telecine operator for television, who came over every evening to light our sets. I can't say enough about Laurie Stewart. Chief Engineer, Mike Hately seemed a rather distant man, not talking much with us. But Laurie Stewart went out of his way to help. Not surprisingly he got married to a Jamaican girl some time later, and put down roots in Jamaica. The JIS staff grew. Audrey Chong and Ken Jones were joined by Martin Mordecai, Mitzie Townsend, Easton Lee, Jeanne Barnes, Freddie Borough, Don Bucknor, Pat Thomas, Richard (Tony) Robinson, Al Scott, among others. One of Jamaica's finest painters, George Rodney, came on for awhile as our artist. But poor George with all his talent, found himself doing mostly captions; so he quit. The staff had a very high morale. We met every week to plan ahead and review the work in hand. Every guest on our programmes was made to feel welcome and comfortable, cup of tea and all that. Because every presentation was basically "live", rehearsals were crucial. We had about an hour of rehearsal time, and everything had to be straightened-out and stream-lined during that period.

In spite of all efforts, unforeseen things would happen during transmission. On one occasion a flat, which was not properly anchored, began to come down on a guest. An alert props-man caught it in time, and an equally alert programme producer (director) quickly switched cameras to conceal the near-accident from viewers. Another time, a nervous guest, not realizing we were on the air, pointed to a cameraman and said: *"Why is he looking at me like that?"*

Perhaps the worst thing was when guests panicked and dried-up. Interviewers were forced to be inventive in order to keep the programme going.

Our television slogan was: *"Watch Jamaica on JIS"*. Programmes began initially at 6:30 pm but were later put to 6:00pm. Whatever the time, most people with a TV tuned in to catch the coat-of-arms backed by the theme tune: *"Gimme Back Me Shilling..."* and was eager to watch Jamaica on JIS. Our first 'live' presentation was the weather report and forecast by the Meteorological Office. Large metal maps of the Caribbean area and Jamaica were acquired, with magnetic symbols representing sun, rain, wind, clouds, temperature, etc. the Weathermen moved the symbols around as they gave their reports and forecasts. The first weathermen were Mike Nancoo and Don Vickers. They were superb. Mike in particular was very engaging, with his swash-buckling approach and refreshing humor. He was from Trinidad, married to a Jamaican girl (Claudette) from Flint River in St. Mary. The Weathermen were Jamaica's first TV stars. One of our earliest programmes was a feature on the Morant Bay Rebellion, using photographs, drawings and maps. It came out of my master's thesis and was a great success.

We felt free to explore and to present a wide range of subjects since the government was involved in all aspects of the country's life; from sports and culture to hard things like agriculture, industry, education and budget. And speaking of budget reminds me of the time, before TV came along, when I virtually elbowed my way into the inner sanctum of the Ministry of Finance, being determined to try to present the country's budget in a simplified form. Officials were aghast, incredulous; that anyone should think it was necessary for ordinary people to gasp the intricacies of the budget; or that it could be subjected to simplification. Finally I was ushered into the 'inner-inner' sanctum, where sat the great man himself, the High Priest, the Financial Secretary. He happened to be the awe-inspiring Edgerton Rudolph Richardson, who became Jamaica's Permanent Representative at the United Nations in 1963 and was later knighted by the Queen and appointed Ambassador to the U.S. But on the day I was "permitted" to enter his office he was Financial Secretary; top man in Jamaica's still prestigious civil service. He looked just short of scornful. There was almost a pained expression on his face when he said: "And who is Mr. Robinson?" That was the same question (more or less) Sir Arthur Lewis had asked, after I "butchered" his radio broadcast on

Independence. As I remember, I was permitted to do a programme on the budget, but I don't know if I improved anybody's understanding of it.

The first "folklore" Jamaican TV programme was a feature we called "Jack Mandora", which was tagged on to either our Saturday or Sunday programme. It was presented by Vernon Lopez, a man with a natural comic, convincing, country-type face, and a courageous laugh. One of his major props was a big bunch of green bananas, which would be tested from time to time to see how it was ripening. Lopez told Anancy Stories and other folk tales, and after awhile we expanded the feature and brought in young people to participate. Jack Mandora was also a huge success, and I remember Mickey Hendricks phoning me and saying he wished he had thought of the idea first. Jamaican officials and experts of all sorts came on JIS. Even Ministers of Government like Edwin Allen. We gave him some knotty questions to answer on his controversial education portfolio. It was a great experience for Jamaican viewers to be in the "company" of people who presided over the vital things which had to be confronted in our newly-independent country, we felt useful and uplifted because we were able to make it possible.

All kinds of talent were featured on JIS. Bob Marley's first television appearance (before he had his locks) was on JIS. We even had the fabled Louise Bennett and Ranny Williams. Archie Moore, one time light-heavyweight boxing champion and heavyweight contender, did a boxing series on JIS. He was in Jamaica on a government-sponsored programme. T.K. Wint (my old physical training teacher at Calabar) took part in a couple of the programmes. He seemed uneasy. A hard-fought battle in the boxing ring was child's play when compared with facing a TV camera.

But perhaps the best-loved performer was burly "Sagwa" Bennett: singer, bass fiddle player, and cigar-smoking comedian.

Sagwa always came on time, rehearsed with great seriousness and gave of his best in every performance.

The JBC engineers (Laurie Stewart, Don Wellington, Rupert Bent, Henry Lowe and Oval Lue), master control (Mervyn Carby, Don Blades, Dickie Fowler and David Daniels) and studio cameramen (Bill Cummings, Alfonso Walker, Winston Hewling, Louis Burke, Ian Edwards, Winston "Stoogie" Hylton, Winston Gibbs, Billy Sheriff and David Aflick) pitched in and supported our efforts with great enthusiasm.

JIS also took the lead with the first Jamaican TV drama series. It was called "Life With The Littles" and featured such acting talent as Bobby Lee, Fitz Weir, Joan McLacklan, Teddy Patel, Karen Harrison, Huntly Alston, Donald Harrison, Bobby Lewis and Jean Bernard. Richard (Tony) Robinson, (son of Mr. M.G. Robinson), was the principal director of the series. Like the radio series ("Corporal Clooney", "Raymond the Spray-man" and "Life in Hopeful Village") "Life With the Littles" was built around messages such as filling out your Income Tax Form. It was good fun, which was done 'live' in the studio, except for an occasional film insert. Viewers loved it. It was definitely something new, seeing Jamaican drama (a cross between a sitcom and a Soap Opera) on TV.

There were times when programmes staggered to the brink of disaster. There was one I remember which required a great number of captions. Unfortunately, too many were crammed unto the caption stands. As the assistant on the studio floor began to change captions, in keeping with the needs of the narration some began to fall. The camera captured mad moments, with the hands of the assistant in vision, desperately trying to put captions in place, falling behind the narration and putting up captions that were no longer relevant. When the producers switched to the narrator (Anthony Hill) to avoid showing the mess, there was the narrator, pausing in mid-sentence and looking positively stunned.

Magnificent JIS-TV

JBC boasted that "never before has a television service been established in so short a period of time". The trouble was that an equal amount of effort and thought was not given to the Jamaican component of the programme schedule. Were we going to be immersed in a deeper ocean of American shows just when we were launching out into independence?

JIS-TV stepped resolutely into the "Jamaican programmes breech", so to speak. My old boss, Evon Blake writing in the Spotlight Magazine of January,1966, said:-

> *"Ask any discerning television viewer in Jamaica what are the best programmes produced on JBC-TV and you will get the answer: the programmes of the Jamaica Information Service. In its half hour slot (6:30 - 7:00pm), JIS packs a wealth of visual material that has top rating.*

> *JIS has become a force in local television and radio. Its wide variety of programmes, running the range of information and entertainment, is high-grade stuff that demand, and gets, high-volume listenership.*

> *Talks, interviews, in-depth reporting, plays, classical music recitals, jazz concerts, panel discussions – all form part of the varied, first-class fare which JIS provides seven nights a week on television. The radio fare is just as varied and of equally high quality.*

Some communications media like to claim the title, "The voice of Jamaica," but if any one agency of information is entitled to be so called it is the Jamaica Information Service. For not only in the area of radio and television, but in the sphere of the press and the cinema as well, JIS comes out, efficiently and effectively..."

I could hardly believe my eyes when I read Evon Blake's enthusiastic praise. But he went even further, describing JIS as:

"a hive of activities of the Government and the Ministries, and distributing these to press, radio and television; providing news coverage of official tours, conference and engagements in publicity matters; assisting visiting journalists, broadcasters and others; providing information; answering enquires from overseas for information, etc."

All I could say was: *"Amen, and Thank you, Evon."*

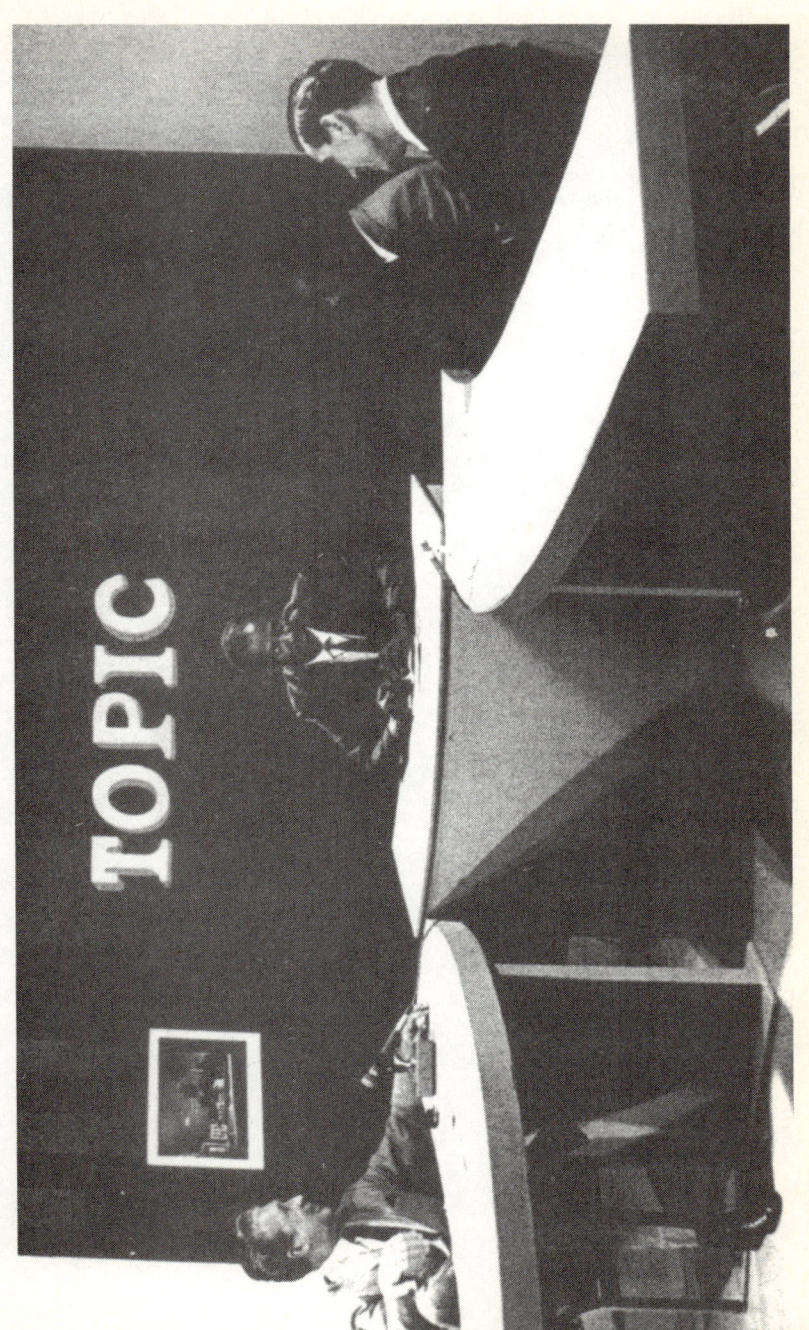

JIS-TV

Work Is Life

On Saturday morning, April 4, 1964, I drove to my office at 124 East Street. We were still working half day on Saturdays. Shortly after I sat down at my desk the telephone rang. I answered and was told that my father had met in an accident. A motorcycle had knocked him down and he had been taken to the Kingston Public Hospital. Someone said he was dead.

I didn't want to move, but I forced myself to get up and drive to the hospital. My father wasn't dead. He was unconscious; bones broken, barely breathing. They took him to a ward, and I sat beside his bed and waited. But I couldn't sit there and just wait for him to die. My sister was living in Jamaica at the time. I drove to her place at Maryland, off the road to Newcastle, and told her what had happened. She went into a kind of 'denial' immediately. Our father would be alright. But when I returned to the hospital he was dead; a sheet pulled up over his head. He had never regained consciousness.

When I was three or four, I watched him catching butterflies with a big, white net. He pressed them between pages in a book, along with various flowers and leaves. I remember going behind him down to a rocky beach in Port Antonio one night, where some fishermen had brought in a huge, strange, "sea creature." Another night I followed him to a morgue where he viewed the corpse of a man whose head had been taken off by a train wheel. My father was a pharmacist and was then attached to the Port

Antonio Hospital. As I grew up I became afraid of him because he never spared the rod. In the evenings when I heard the scrape of the metal front gate and knew he was home, I made myself scarce. His countenance towards me always seemed severe. I was sure he didn't like me. Yet I never lacked for anything; and if we got sick he would quickly mix-up some kind of medicine which would make us feel better in no time. He was a pharmaceutical genius. And I was aware that everyone respected him.

Shortly after my father's death some senior pharmacists informed me of a decision to name a new room in the pharmacy section of the Kingston Public Hospital after him. I was elated. But it never happened. Someone sabotaged the idea and it was quickly dropped. I was outraged.

He was a man of absolute integrity: totally reliable and committed to his work; intolerant of low standards and loose speech. In one of his notebooks I found a clipping which said:-

> *"The greatest pleasure we get out of life is through the work we do. Work, if performed in the proper spirit gives more pleasure than play. The joy of accomplishment that goes with it is a very great pleasure indeed. The road to happiness lies through much work, well done."*

That seemed to be my father's creed. In fact he was on his way to work, three days short of his 79th birthday when he was struck down. I never got close to him except through letters he wrote to me when I was a student. To counter the shock and depression brought about by my father's death, I turned again to play-writing. Again the subject came out of my historical research: the career of Maroon Chief Cudjoe. The play was called "Mountain Lion" and I entered it in the drama competition of the 1964 Jamaica Festival.

The night when "Mountain Lion" was being put on in the eliminations at the Little Theatre, we went all about the neighbourhood, pulling wild vines from fences to be used as set dressing. Under the stage lights the vine covered sets emerged dramatically and gave the feeling of being outdoors in the untamed bush. Buddy Pouyatt who had played the runaway slave in "The Runaway" took the part of Cudjoe in "Mountain Lion" and did a tremendous job. The whole cast was great, and the play made it to the finals in Montego Bay.

Transportation was provided but I drove over in my own car with some of the cast as I intended to return that night. In Montego Bay we again gathered wild vines for our sets; and once again the audience was transported into Maroon bush country. We won first prize. In fact we won nine awards out of ten, (I think) including best set. We put on bathing suits, jumped in the pool at the hotel reserved for accommodation, and swam joyfully about. Then I got into my car with two or three others and drove back to Kingston, arriving in the very early morning "dead tired". I was back at my desk at the usual time.

The JBC Strike

When JBC was launched in 1959, the Chief Minister, Norman Manley (not yet Premier) sat side by side with Herbert McDonald at a small organ in the big radio studio. McDonald was showing Mr. Manley how the organ worked, pumping the pedal with his feet and playing a few notes. Mr. Manley tried it afterwards, to the delight of everyone present. The Chief Minister was in a good mood and clearly happy with everything. His dream of a Broadcasting Corporation to serve Jamaica had apparently become a reality.

It was obvious to me that the JBC staff regarded Norman Manley as the founder/father of the Corporation. There was (what we in these times would call) a "DNA link" from parent to child which was permanent. When he lost the elections of 1962 they felt "orphaned". How could the children now turn with welcoming arms to those who had caused them to be orphaned? The aura which had surrounded the Camelot of broadcasting began to dim. The Corporation's new chairman, K.H. Ivan Levy, and his Board, seemed like conquering barbarians taking charge of a falling city. Before long, a sort of defiant spirit began to emerge which fed on Mickey Hendricks' uncertainty about how the Corporation should relate to a confident new government.

After the elections, Hendricks had said at a Broadcasting Conference in Canada, that JBC was enshrined in a law which ruled out ministerial interference. His claim that JBC was free to criticize the Government and battle with it, if needs be, on matters of principle, was greeted with cynicism. The records showed that in 1959, after a little less than a year in operation, JBC lost about 76,000 pounds; in 1960, 82,000 pounds, in 1961, a little over 70,000; in 1962 and 1963, about 60,000 pounds each year. With its commitment to "the life and growth of the nation" and its somewhat starry-eyed beginnings, those results were not unexpected. But it meant that JBC was becoming more and more obligated to government, which "bailed it out" each year. And there is a well-known saying that "he who pays the piper calls the tune." The fact that Government appointed the Corporation's Chairman and Board inevitably added to the dilemma.

By 1963 Mickey Hendricks was running into trouble. Time after time he felt impelled to ask Morris Cargill, popular press and radio commentator, to alter scripts which appeared to be too critical of the government, or Government Ministers. On one occasion Cargill said: "I do not think Mr. Allen (the Minister of Education) has been a success as a minister. "He was asked to add a word that would take some of the edge off the criticism. Another time he said that Minister Allen "had a habit of speaking endlessly, repetitiously and boringly." He was asked to cut out "repetitiously" and "boringly." A script he wrote about an incident involving Rastafarians at Coral Gardens was held up, because it contained criticisms of government's handling of a colour incident at the Kingston Sheraton Hotel involving a U.S. citizen. He said:

"I cannot continue to broadcast in an atmosphere that chokes me with timidity and vacillation, and above all, with the kind of hypocrisy which pretends in public that I am given reasonable freedom when, in private, every kind of obstruction is used to see that I don't get it. It has become obvious to me that the policy of JBC (or perhaps I should be more accurate to

say the policy of Mickey Hendricks) has been to discourage as much as possible any meaningful criticism of Government."

Cargill went across to RJR. He was very popular and the incident dealt a severe blow to JBC's credibility. It was also a hard body-blow to Hendricks, who had come up from RJR in 1961 with exciting high hopes. He was naïve, thinking that, with his background in the hard, pragmatic commercial world of RJR, he could cope with a "politically manufactured" organization which came to be regarded by many as one of the spoils of political warfare. But Hendricks was not alone. The majority of us in the "business" were naïve and starry-eyed in those hopeful days, believing that what was required of us was high-minded professionalism and a maximum use of talents.

In addition to the "defection" of Cargill to the arch rival at 32 Lyndhurst Road, there were more questions when the controversial John Maxwell was dismissed from the JBC news room. Young John of my Gleaner days had developed into a hard-hitting journalist, who made some people in the temporary seats of power uneasy.

Peter Abrahams and Frank Hill, two respected personalities in the field of journalism, were hired as commentators on JBC-TV, and this gave things a boost. However, the staff, apparently feeling the need for a buffer against the new Board, joined the National Workers Union (NWU) which had sprung out of Norman Manley's PNP. In October 1963, an agreement was reached between the Corporation and the NWU to increase wages. But the Government announced that any revenue made by JBC should go, in the first instance, to the re-payment of a loan which had been guaranteed by government. An increase in wages and salaries would obviously cut down on JBC's ability to repay the loan. As a result, the Corporation offered to increase the wages and salaries for sub-ordinate staff and typists, but for no one else.

On January 27, 1964, JBC carried a story on the union negotiations. It was written by George Lee of the newsroom who was a union delegate. Adrian Rodway, the editor in charge, passed it for broadcast. It was felt that the story was biased and in favour of the union. The next day both Lee and Rodway were fired.

The Editorial and Technical staff went on strike. Freelancers withdrew their services. Soon about one hundred and twenty people were out on strike, including some announcers. As was the case with RJR and their strike, several years before, the Corporation managed to stay on the air. An attempt was made to classify JIS-TV and Radio staff as "strike breakers" when they continued to produce and broadcast their programmes. But JIS wasn't about to be intimidated. After a while they left us alone.

The handful of JBC programmes staff who remained at their posts were threatened and severely harassed. This was only to be expected. Some of the technical staff who were on strike, managed to sabotage the equipment, and the station was off the air for a of couple hours. But the engineers soon got things working again. An attempt was made to frighten off advertisers, but without much success.

The strike soon reached bitter proportions. The "privileged" strikers, unaccustomed to the hard-rock business of being out on the streets, and disconcerted by the fact that the station was continuing to broadcast, became furious. They lay down in front of the JBC gates so no vehicles could drive through. They lay down on the hot asphalt roads at Half-Way-Tree and on King's Street, and blocked traffic. Some of them really thought they were involved in some "nation saving" exercise, and abandoned themselves to their new and exciting roles. They used cars to block traffic on Windward Road. They tried marching without permission, but the police scattered them with tear gas. They got some support from workers in other organizations, like Cable and Wireless, where staff refused to handle messages and material for JBC.

The press gave good coverage to the sensational "middle-class" strike, so different from the usual blue-collar, rough–handed strikes. But some citizens, who were at first sympathetic, soon became annoyed when the traffic blockers got in the way of work and business. The young "intellectuals" on the Mona Campus of the University of The West Indies were eager to plunge into the fray. It gave them an opportunity to demonstrate that they were alive to the issues of the day. They marched down from campus and went through Jamaica College to avoid the police. JC boys shielded them. Their headmaster, Harvey Ennevor, was deputy chairman of JBC, and was often absent from the school because of the troubles.

Mickey Hendricks had experienced the RJR strike and it was not as virulent as JBC's, because it didn't have the political components. At RJR it had just been a conflict between workers and managements. But at JBC, one could see the shadows of the two opposing political parties looming on each side. At JBC, the one or two members of the announcing staff still on the job began to both announce and operate. But the savagery of the conflict had worn down Mickey Hendricks. The magic and promise had gone out of his job. The atmosphere in the board room and at meetings held elsewhere, was grim. The Chairman, K.H. Ivan Levy, dug in and held firm. There were disloyal elements among the staff who were determined to overturn the Corporation, they would have to do it over his dead body. Henry Fowler, the sole survivor from the old PNP Board, resigned. Nobody was surprised. Sylvia Wynter Carew took his place.

As the JIS representative on the Board, I was able to observe everything from the inside. I was fascinated by the struggle. I watched Ivan Levy at those tense Board meetings, as he sipped tea or coffee and smoked endlessly. I couldn't help but admire his fortitude. To the militant staff outside he was the dragon, and they were howling for his blood. But he was committed to his responsibilities as Chairman and he endured the heat; tight-lipped, his grey-green eyes serious and resolute. In spite of the savage confrontations, the NWU was getting nowhere. They decided to go to arbitration, but demanded that Lee and Rodway be reinstated if their dismissal was found to be unjustified. JBC demanded that the union's reinstatement demand be struck out. There was an indication that the private sector supported the JBC stand. Just when it seemed that an agreement was about to be reached, Ivan Levy fell sick. Behind his implacable exterior, the strain had taken its toll. He was out for a while and the Deputy Chairman, Harvey Ennevor, Headmaster of JC (Jamaica College) acted as chairman. Ennevor was a tall, dapper, elegant, well-spoken man, a fit representative of the old style, conservative JC image. He kept things going until Ivan Levy (very shortly) was back. In March (1964), the Ministry of Labour appointed Donald Eccleston, a Puisne Judge, to be a one man Board of Enquiry into the dispute. JBC stuck by its determination not to re-employ Lee and Rodway. Somewhere towards the end of the ninety-seven day strike, Mickey Hendricks resigned. Staff who had remained at their posts felt they had been deserted. Harvey Ennevor took over that tremendously "hot seat" as general manager. But the wear and tear was also affecting the strikers. Many of them just wanted to get back to work and get on with their lives. Had it been worth all that fury? To a section of the public the thing had just become an annoyance.

One day, before the dispute was settled, a popular, veteran announcer, who was out on strike, walked boldly through the JBC gates and said he wanted to go back to work. He was told he would have to wait until the matter was resolved. By the time the strike ended, any immediate hope that the wounds could be speedily healed, and the Corporation be unified once more with a common purpose, was gone. For almost a year, some returning strikers refuse to speak to the handful of programme staff who had chosen to remain at their posts. A spirit of disaffection continued to haunt the JBC.

The young hot-bloods never gave deep thought to what they were doing. They were cheerfully swept away by emotion and did not ponder the root causes. The strike may have seemed like a righteous crusade, but in fact, it contributed significantly to the polarization of the Jamaican society. Thirty years later, the hot-blooded youths, now become middle-aged people sitting in their grilled St. Andrew residences, would bemoan the tribalization of the Jamaican society and wonder how it came about. They would blame corrupt, uncaring officials; greedy politicians; garrison communities; dons and inner-city backwardness. They would not recognize the part they had played.

In the forefront, background and in the midst of the strikers, was the compelling figure of Senator Michael Manley, first Vice President and Island Supervisor of the National Workers Union. He still had his disarming smile. But in the heat of the strike there was also something fierce, which I thought I detected when he stood on the sideline at Jamaica College, watching the rough-house Calabar team going by at half time.

Falling Down And Getting Up

In the midst of the uncertainties and pressures, JIS moved from 124 East Street, a place I had passionately disliked. It found new quarters nearby, in the old Banana Board building at 10 South Avenue, Kingston Gardens. It was not as run-down, and we had more rooms; more parking space. But when we had cleaned it up and organized ourselves, we realized that it could only be an interim solution.

Also in the midst of the burgeoning events, I developed a fever. My temperature rose higher each day. I rapidly lost strength and had to stay home. Drawing on ignorant concepts of treatment, I covered-up each night when my temperature rose, "to sweat out the fever." It didn't work, of course. My aunt, Dorothy DuVerney, who was a nurse, called in a doctor. He couldn't figure out what was wrong, but thought I might have hepatitis. The doctors got me admitted to the University Hospital and they put me in Ward 8. I had a room to myself. They gave me all kinds of tests but I didn't pay attention to anything. I lay immobile. I refused to see any visitors, which alarmed the nurses. Some relatives, friends and colleagues sent me get-well cards and flowers. I ignored all of that. I felt as if I didn't want to live. My wife and little daughter were a slender thread that kept me connected to existence. The hospital people finally told me I had pneumonia. I was sure it was just an effect. I felt absolutely ridiculous one day when I was taken in a wheelchair to the laboratory. In my growing up days

I had been a dedicated physical culture buff. Now I was being wheeled around; a wretched, pathetic weakling. The nurse eased and coaxed me hoping to restore my interest in life. A female physiotherapist came in occasionally and pounded my back violently. Slowly I began to return to the land of the living. Finally, having received medical approval, I struggled into my clothes, staggered out of Ward 8 and was taken home.

As soon as I was strong enough I went back to work; back into the thick of things. I hadn't learned very much from my ordeal but the "rest" had done me some good. My belly aches were gone.

Digging For History

Early in the 20th century, an Englishman headmaster at Calabar High School was asked by a young Jamaican teacher why Jamaican history was not taught. He said: "My boy, you have no history." In the 1920s a Jamaican politician got up in the Legislative Council in Headquarters House and pleaded for the teaching of Jamaican history in schools. He was ridiculed and torn to shreds by the editor of a daily newspaper.

In the 1950s while I was working at Radio Jamaica, Peter Orr, my colleague announcer (a young Englishman and a Cambridge graduate) looked at me sadly and shook his head in the negative, when the subject of Jamaican history came up. He assured me that Jamaican history could only be seen as an appendage of British history. During the same period a Canadian history teacher at Hampton High School (then a prestigious school for girls) opposed to the teaching of Jamaican history. *"After all,"* she said, *"Jamaica is only a dot on the map of the British empire."* Another headmaster of Calabar (an Australian) said he objected to the teaching of Jamaican history because *"it showed up England in a bad light over the slave trade."* It was alright for Australians to know about the transportation of "convicts" from Britain to Australia, but Jamaicans must forever be kept in the dark about themselves.

But of course, when people live together for generations they acquire a history. They may lose much of it however, if they do not make a conscious effort to research and document it. So

Independent Jamaica got to work to dig for its history in the 1960s, and to reinterpret and re-evaluate the facts and events.

1965 was the 100th anniversary of the Morant Bay Rebellion, a major turning point in the history of Jamaica, which threw up two men (George William Gordon and Paul Bogle) who, like Marcus Garvey, were to be made National Heroes. Vic Reid, novelist and one-time Gleaner reporter, had grappled with the subject in his book "New Day." Now it was time for an in-depth historical look.

A rather eccentric little American named Ray Fremmer got the go-ahead from the authorities to locate the remains of rebels and others connected to the 1865 rebellion. Fremmer lived in a decaying house on Green Park Estate in Trelawny. He was an amateur archaeologist, and later gained the reputation for being a daring raider of historical relics. He collected grave stones and other artifacts from all over the place, and deposited them in the yard at Green Park. Fremmer used the testimony of a suspected rebel prisoner named John Grant, which was published in 1866. Grant and eleven others had been forced to dig pits in which to bury executed prisoners. Fremmer found three pits on the second day of his search, and three others later. Seventy-nine skeletons were exposed in a row of adjoining pits at the fort behind the Court House at Morant Bay. Fremmer was deeply moved. The crowds that surrounded the pits every day stood in stunned silence. During the three weeks of digging about two thousand people visited the site. Three pits were in an old refuse dump behind the wall of the fort. John Grant and the eleven others dug three feet for the first pit, and then were apparently ordered to stop.

The first pit contained sixteen skeletons, neatly laid head to toe. In the last five pits (in contrast to the first), the bodies had been laid facing in any direction. Some skeletons were lying on top of one another. The majority of the skulls were crushed out of shape, probably because of the clay which holds water and becomes the heaviest type of soil. Shirt and trousers buttons were found and two chalk pipes with broken stems. There were very few skulls with teeth missing, and no cavities were found in any teeth. Except for one skeleton, whose owner had apparently been suffering from Paget's Disease, no deformities were found.

I was shocked when I heard that all the bones were eventually lumped together and put into a pit by the fort. A rather insignificant-looking monument was placed over this common grave to mark the spot where the remains of seventy-nine of those executed at the Morant Bay Court House (including Gordon and Bogle) were laid. Apart from selecting a design for a monument to Gordon and Bogle, and erecting a monument in the National Shrine, (based on the winning design), the government's major offering in commemorating the centenary of the Morant Bay Rebellion was a stage play, called "Ballad for a Rebellion". A large cast was assembled, which included some of the best actors in Jamaica. No money was spared in the acquisition of sets and the proper costumes. The best lighting and make-up experts were recruited. Rehearsals were intense and there was a good deal of publicity.

The script was written by Sylvia Wynter, who had all the relevant material in the Institute of Jamaica and its West India Reference Library (now the National Library of Jamaica) at her disposal to take home if she wanted to. Young Lloyd Reckford a Jamaican living in the U.K. was brought down to direct the play. I didn't see how I could possibly stand on the sidelines and not make some significant contribution to this event. It seemed that my many months of research at Howard, culminating in my master's thesis on the Morant Bay Rebellion, had been done unwittingly for this occasion. And of course, I had hosted that well-received documentary on the rebellion on JIS-TV, shortly after we had gone on the air.

I had to get in there with my own version. But how? The answer came loud and clear. Make a film. I had written many dramatized radio plays and a couple of stage plays, one of which (Mountain Lion) had won nine awards in the 1964 annual festival. But I had never made a film. And we had no money to make a film.

Time Of Fury

At first I thought we should just do a short, simple film; like a re-enactment of the fight outside the Morant Bay Court House between Bogle's people and the volunteers. This was the fateful clash that started the chain of action which culminated in the surrender of the old Jamaican Constitution and the establishment of Crown Colony Government in 1866. But, as I sat and brooded about how to bring it to life, the whole thing just began to grow and grow, until I found myself writing a script for a full-length film. Sylvia Wynter was kind enough to lend me some of the material from the library for a few nights. What was extremely useful was the evidence given to the Royal Commission sent out by the British Government to investigate the whole affair. I did all the work at night, after my regular work-day, and I hardly slept as I went through the voluminous report and made notes.

There was a regular annual allocation in the JIS budget for films to be made by the film unit. I dipped cautiously into it, and, one day we just started to shoot. The rationale was that the film would be just one of a number of films that would be made during the year, which would be used on television and on the mobile Cinema Units of the JIS. But in the "back of my head" was the hope that it would be an important educational tool that could probably be used for years. In my growing up days I had been profoundly influenced by historical films such as "The Crusades", "The Last Days of Pompeii", "Clive of India" and "The Charge of the Light Brigade". Why shouldn't we try to bring to life one of the most dramatic and significant events in the history of our country, where the heroes were our own people?

The lack of resources just had to be overcome. We looked with longing at the magnificent costumes being assembled for the stage play, (Ballad for a Rebellion), the authentic military uniforms of the period, imported straight from Britain, or so we had heard. There was not a hope in the world that we would be permitted to borrow some of them. So we started to scrounge; to beg and borrow (but not to steal) from every possible source. When we couldn't find what we wanted, we bought cheap cloth, and put a dressmaker to work.

One of the biggest problems was to find out what the uniform of the volunteers who fought at the Court House was like. We researched, and looked at the old photos and prints of the 1860's and finally came up with something that proved to be pretty near. Zouave uniforms for the First West India Regiment were more easily obtained. The Jamaica Military Band still wore them. We got hold of some "cast off" uniforms, and the band-men and some policemen played the parts.

Uniforms for the British Soldiers of the Sixth Royal Regiment almost defeated us. We couldn't find any pith helmets of the period. Headgear for the rank and file was nowhere to be seen in Jamaica. Using military period-pictures, we had something made by some enterprising person: cardboard covered with cloth. Its approximately the real thing, but we never pretended it was satisfactory. For weapons we got some old guns which were rusting away in the police armory. But where would we get horses? We had to have horses.

Young Dennis Lalor, who was a polo player, used his own horse and did a scene for us as a mounted messenger, racing to warn the volunteers at the Court House of the approach of

Bogle's men. As he rode over some rough ground towards the camera the horse's hoof hit a protusion and it stumbled and nearly fell; but Dennis "reined him up." One horse wasn't enough, however. We needed many for the mounted soldiers.

Luckily for us the police mounted troop was just being formed. I think they were using retired race horses. Their trainer was Superintendent Ralph Cave of the Royal Canadian Mounted Police, who had been seconded to the Jamaican Police Force for the purpose. Cave was a well built, sinewy six-footer with a keen sense of adventure. When he heard of our plight he was happy to help. The Commissioner of Police at the time was Gordon Langdon, an imposing man. He kindly agreed to put Cave and the newly-formed mounted troop at our disposal. We were eternally grateful to Gordon Langdon.

We also needed trained men to play the part of Maroons and soldiers of the First West Indian Regiment, which were part of the Colonial Forces sent into the East to crush the rebellion. The Brigadier in charge of the Jamaica Defence Force flatly refused to help us. He wasn't going to have anything to do with any re-enactment of the rebellion. But Gordon Longdon again agreed to help us. A lot of rain fell in October, 1865, at the time of the Rebellion. The commanding officer of the Sixth Royals described the mud through which his men had to slog, and the swollen rivers they encountered. For a mad moment we thought of getting the Fire Brigade to use their hoses to simulate rain falling on our actors, as they marched along a narrow trail and through a river. But we stopped short of that. What would happen if a fire broke out while the Fire Brigade was busy wetting down our "troops"? Many years later I wished we had made use of the fire hoses. But surely the simulated heavy rain would have ruined the cardboard headgear of our "British" soldiers.

We were lucky to get some of Jamaica's finest actors, such as Keith Sasso (who played George William Gordon), Rooney

Chambers (Governor Eyre), Bobby Lee (Moses Bogle). We started out with burly Buddy Pouyatt as Paul Bogle; but towards the end of the production, things took a sudden and unexpected turn, which caused us to lose Buddy and endangered the entire effort. The part of the German Baron, Von Ketelholdt was played by Klaus Markens, a young Geman living in Jamaica, who got married to our first Miss World, Carol Joan Crawford. Our Royal Canadian Mounty, Superintendent Ralph Cave, played the part of Major General Forbes Jackson, a retired Indian Army Officer, who attached himself to the Sixth Royals, and ran into Paul Bogle by a river one day.

A lady from the Tourist Board volunteered to do "makeup," she soon disappeared, and never returned. Our actors helped to put make-up on each other, and saw to it that costumes looked alright on one another. Keith Sasso, a veteran thespian, was especially helpful in this respect. Sometimes they had to mend holes and rips in well-used costumes, and improvise neck-cloths. We didn't have enough money to pay anybody a decent fee. Sometimes it seemed that our "big stars" were working for little more than patties and aerated water, and a sandwich now and then. Every time we shot a scene we worried about how much we were eating into the annual film budget. Everyday we wondered if some bureaucrat would suddenly descend on us and demand to know who had authorized the project. We were so hard-up that if anything went wrong with a crowd scene we couldn't shoot over. People chosen for the crowds were solemnly ordered to wear old clothes; and for the women, long skirts. But, inevitably, a few would-be Hollywood stars would turn up wearing new pants with seams pressed to a knife-edge, and the latest in sports shirts. Some women would appear in very short skirts, or wearing their Sunday-best hats. Occasionally we wouldn't notice some of these aberrations until after the scene was shot. The crowd had to be paid on the spot, and there was no money left over for a re-take. So the editor (Dudley Harrison) would have to work doubly hard to save the scene.

I remember a young boy named Neville Polack, who was part of a crowd which was watching George William Gordon being taken to his execution. The crowd was instructed to look "sad" but every time the tracking camera went past Polack he would break into a smile. He just couldn't help himself. The footage had to be dumped.

Most of the Court House fight was filmed in Morant Bay, in front of the Court House (Bogle's statue wasn't there yet), inside the building, and in the rear. We had to shoot some additional action so we went back one day with our volunteers, armed and in their uniforms. But we hadn't done much when Franklyn (Chappie) St. Juste, our main cameraman, dropped his camera. He tried to fix it, but couldn't; so we had to pack up and return to Kingston.

Chappie St. Juste worked very hard to make that difficult, ground breaking production come off. He set up a night scene at Port Royal, so we could film the culmination of the Court House fight; coming up with a spinning contraption which, when placed in front of a light, created the appearance of flickering flames. He came up with a model of a wooden house which, when set on fire, looked like a full-sized house burning. I remember him crouched in the river-water with a camera firmly held, filming Superintendent Ralph Cave galloping straight at him through the water, I thought the horse was going to run over him. Then there was the day we filmed Paul Bogle being chased by Ralph Cave, as General Forbes Jackson; both on horse-back. They were to ride along a narrow, winding path in the Kintyre Area. Cave lent us his station wagon. The back was opened out and Chappie lay on the floor of the wagon as it sped over the narrowing trail, rolling his camera at the police "stunt man" playing Bogle, and

Inspector Cave, galloped swiftly after the vehicle. The wagon rocked around sharp bends, and in spite of skillful driving, hit a protruding rock at one corner; and a little further along, hit another rock at another corner. The left hand side of the wagon which faced the rocky bank of the trail was dented. Where on earth would we find money to repair it? But Cave wouldn't take a cent from us. He repaired it himself.

Before the riding scene began, Cave was asked to start on a rickety bridge over a deep gorge, with the river flowing far below. We were warned that the bridge might not be able to bear the weight of the horse and rider. I suggested that Cave start at the end of it. But the Inspector slowly backed his horse on to the bridge for several yards, even though it creaked and swayed ominously. When he got the signal to go he lashed his horse and thundered away. He fired four shots at "Bogle" three in the scene just before the chase, and one when he gave up the chase and fired as Bogle disappeared over a rise. Of course they were all blank shots, which Cave him self made for the purpose.

There was another uneasy moment when we filmed the scene in which one of Bogle's men climbed to the roof of the Court House and set it on fire with a torch. It was shot at the police premises on Elleston Road, where there was a building with a shingle roof which resembled the one on the old Morant Bay Court House. The Superintendent wasn't happy about it and consented reluctantly. What if the torch should set fire to his roof! As the scene was being shot he was in and out of his office; obviously uneasy but not wanting to appear too worried; staring intently at the man on the roof waving the burning torch. He was obviously relieved when the short scene was finished. No re-takes for that one. One day, we hired a freelance cameraman. After he had set up his camera he called me aside and said: *"Carey, you think we ought to be making this kind of a film?"*

For a moment I was taken a back and didn't know what to say. I understood the Brigadier's bias. He was aware that if he could possibly have been head of the armed forces in 1865 (which given the circumstances of the time he could never have been), he might have gone out and butchered and terrorized the people of eastern Jamaica, as Governor Eyre's men had done. He would have had a duty. However, this cameraman was just like the rest of us, but without a flicker of understanding. When the film was quite far advanced I felt I had to bring the Minister fully into the proceedings. I had been working late at nights with the editor, Dudley Harrison. We worked in the old dilapidated building at the corner of Hanover and North Streets, often into the early hours of the morning. Dudley put the shots and scenes together with ancient "film cement", and sometimes the film would come apart as we viewed it. The Minister, Edward Seaga, was very interested, but he didn't come down right away. He sent Sylvia Wynter to look at it. Then he sent a committee of his cultural gurus, some of whom were associated with Sylvia's play, "Ballad for a Rebellion". That was perhaps a psychological mistake. We were potential rivals.

One of the gurus was a man I had admired as an outspoken champion in the cause of responsible nationhood. I asked him what he thought of the "rough cut" of the film; and he said if the government had intended to make a film, they should have engaged the services of one of the big name film-makers from overseas. I was shocked... I still had not grasped the extent of the slavish mentality of many Jamaicans, including some who appeared to be liberated.

I hesitated to think what would have happened to the story in the hands of a Cecil B. DeMille, aided by a Hollywood scriptwriter. How would Gordon and Bogle have emerged, especially with Charlton Heston playing Governor Eyre. And what would the production have cost? The film would just never have been made.

I was bolstered by some ancient Roman sayings:-

"What one has, one ought to use: and whatever he does he should do with all his might."

"Courage desires no foreign aid; is full of life by her own resources."

"In great enterprises, to have attempted is enough."

According to Ralph Waldo Emerson: "The world leaves every man to set his own value. It will accept your own measure of your doing and being".

Having listened to his gurus and advisers, the Minister finally came down to see the rough-cut of the film. He sat by himself in a darkened room. I hovered in the background.

Dudley Harrison rolled the film on the noisy projector. In spite of strengthening the weak spots with the ancient "cement," the film began to break, every now and then. I sweated. Dudley did a quick "wrap around" of the film every time it broke, and then took up more or less where we left off. Each time the film broke I expected to see the Minister get up and leave in disgust. But he sat there patiently, and silently watched the whole of it.

At the end he stood up, looking very thoughtful, as if staring into his own mind. Finally he said he would call me. Then he thanked everybody and left. I felt we had lost the game. The next day the Minister telephoned. He said he didn't think Buddy Pouyatt looked sufficiently like Paul Bogle. That was a devastating blow, as Buddy was 'centrestage' in a significant part of the film. Discouraged, I offered to scrap the project and just show bits and pieces on television. The Minister said, "No, try and find another Paul Bogle." That seemed like an impossible task. We only had a few weeks to finish the film if we were to meet the deadline for the commemoration.

When I talked it over with my colleagues someone suggested we try a young actor named Uriel Aldridge. Keith Sasso said we could "age" him with make-up. I sent photographs of Uriel to the Minister, who said he looked more like Bogle but seemed a little too young. I said we would "age" him. With just a few weeks to go we had to shoot over just about all the scenes in which Buddy appeared, assembling all the cast involved and going back to the locations. Then we had to process and edit the film. Dudley Harrison didn't get more than four hours sleep each night for more than a week, and neither did I. We huddled over the editing equipment, night after night, trying to keep awake. But we just made it, and rushed the film off to England for the final work to be done. Dudley went up too.

Nigeria

I was now scheduled to attend a Commonwealth Broadcasting Conference in Nigeria, as one of a two-member delegation from JBC. Merrick Needham was going as general manager and I, as a board member, and leader of the delegation. I was exhausted and didn't want to go. Everybody thought I was crazy to think of missing such an opportunity. Today, I am glad they practically "forced" me to go. I would never have gotten another chance to visit Nigeria.

I got off the plane at London airport suffering from both jet-lag and post-production fatigue. My big blue bag could not be found and there was no one to meet me. I took the airport bus to the bus terminus, phoned the Hyde Park Hotel and was told they had a room reserved for me. I linked up with Merrick Needham at the hotel, which was said to be a "high class" establishment. It was full of stiff-looking types. Ignoring my state of fatigue, Merrick took me sight-seeing right away. But first I had to buy some clothes as, with my blue bag missing, I only had what I was standing in. It was a Saturday so we had to run for an underground train in order to get to a clothing store before it closed at 1pm. Then I was taken on a brisk tour by Merrick to the House of Parliament, St. James' Palace, the Mall, the Thames Embankment, Piccadilly Circus, Trafalgar Square, the Imperial War Museum, St. James Park and the changing of the Guard at Buckingham Palace.

We had lunch at a "working man's" pub the next day; a cheese sandwich and a pint of half-and-half. One of the patrons looked hard at me and said to his companions: *"Those Jamaicans, there is more of them over here now than there is over where they come from."* But I loved the convivial feel of the pub, and the warm half-and half beer tasted good. That afternoon we took a train to Windsor, saw the Castle and dined with an English family. The big blue bag with my clothes arrived the day I was leaving for Nigeria.

In Nigeria we stopped first at Kano, then went to Lagos, the capital. I found it to be a big, fast-growing place, situated on an island and joined to the mainland by a great bridge which ran over a lagoon. All the country around was flat; not a hill in sight. We lived and held sessions at the Federal Palace Hotel, where the African presence was very strong. The Nigerians wore their national costume or European clothes, as the mood took them, and we strode around with conscious confidence. There was still a considerable European presence, but it seemed almost muted.

When we arrived I was morose, almost depressed; I sunk into myself and did not fraternize with the other delegates. The British coordinator of the conference was concerned, but I soon got out of that mood. The tremendous experience of being in an African country broke open the shell of depression and fatigue. Each delegate was given a car, a driver, and a university student to act as guide. I went to the museum, walked along the bare, hot beach, and ate a meal at the Chinese restaurant which didn't go down well. A mounted troop rode past the Federal Palace Hotel, with guidon and all; looking very smart. The palace seemed to be full of politicians. I found I liked the "ordinary" people more than what appeared to be the ruling class. On Sunday night one of the Nigerian delegates and his wife took us to a place called the Crystal Palace. There I heard a band playing music that sounded "Latin."

It was called "High Life". The Nigerian who took us was a priest, but he was a most extraordinary one. He had a dangerous-looking, roguish face. There he was, drinking beer and dancing to the "High Life" at the Crystal Palace on a Sunday night. After completing our seven-day meeting at Lagos we flew to Enugu in Eastern Nigeria and stayed at the Presidential Hotel, which was much better than the Federal Palace. The African presence at the Presidential seemed less exuberant. The old British colonial presence prevailed. We visited the Niger Bridge at Onitsha, sixty-seven miles from Enugu. They had been working on it for four years and it was nearly finished. It was almost a mile long.

We went to a market in Onitsha; a fabulous, colourful place with all kinds of foodstuffs, craft items and trinkets. I wanted to buy some trinkets but our guide was moving at a fast pace, so I only had time to buy three bananas, one of which I gave away. We left Enugu for Jos flying on a chartered plane, which I think belonged to Pan Africa Airlines. It was an ancient plane. Everybody was nervous because as the aircraft vibrated, screws and bolts seemed to be dropping out, and the door was hanging loose.

Jos is high country, about four thousand feet above sea level, and reminded me of parts of Jamaica. Some of the delegates were put up in the Catering Rest House. Others (including myself) went to the Hill Station Hotel, a lovely old relic of the colonial past. The British used to come here for a rest in the "good old days" and formal traditions still survived. The staff looked and dressed like "house boys." And men had to wear jacket and tie to dinner. There was a near "mutiny" by the Ghanan delegation over the jacket and tie requirement.

We left Jos and went to Kaduna, the capital of Northern Nigeria. We stayed at Hamdala Hotel, overlooking the city's race course. There appeared to be a strong Muslim influence at

Kaduna. Through my hotel window I saw troops drilling on the race course. We wound up the business of the conference at Kaduna, and visited the Governor, Sir Kashim Ibrahim, at State House. I was chosen to make a speech.

Addressing our high-ranking host, I deplored the almost totally negative picture of the continent of Africa that people in my part of the world had been brought up on. A picture which came primarily from "Tarzan" movies, which showed Africa as a place of unrelieved jungles inhabited by savage tribes, with wild animals roaming everywhere. We were fortunate to have come on this trip, where we were able to receive enlightenment. My colleagues applauded loudly, and our distinguished host was very pleased. On the lighter side, I met a very beautiful young woman at a cocktail party, who was the focus of attention. She was alleged to be the mistress of "the ruler of Ghana," and was said to be an Egyptian. "Shades of Cleopatra." I earned the envy of my surprised colleagues when she invited me to have lunch with her the following day.

Nigeria had more than 250 tribal languages and three or four main ones. Broadcasts had to be done in several languages. I remember remarking to the priest with the rough face, who introduced me to "High Life", that it must be rather difficult to maintain unity with so many languages. He was not very happy with my remark. But years later, when Civil War broke out, I was not too surprised.

I left Nigeria for London on September 30, anxious to learn how the film "Time of Fury" had turned out, and whether all would be ready in time for the commemoration of the centenary of the Morant Bay Rebellion.

The Premiere Of "Fury"

The staging of "A Ballard for a Rebellion" was a glittering theatrical and social occasion. It was sponsored by Carreras of Jamaica Ltd, so money was hardly a problem. Two of "Fury's" principals (Keith Sasso and Uriel Aldridge) were in the play, but in different roles. JIS published a first-rate brochure on the play, and the Jamaica Archives in Spanish Town mounted an exhibition of official documents related to the rebellion. All the important and beautiful people seemed to be on the invitation list. But what of "Fury?"

On October 12, nearly two weeks after my return from Nigeria, our Minister announced the completion of the film. He dignified it as the first full-length movie (about one and a half hours) to be produced in Jamaica by Jamaicans; the first of its kind attempted in the island. "Fury" was launched at the Premiere Cinema in Half-Way-Tree (it is no longer there) on Saturday night, October 30, 1965. The Governor General, Sir Clifford Campbell, and Lady Campbell, headed an audience of specially invited guests. The entire Mounted Police of the Jamaica Constabulary was invited. They had been "Fury's" enthusiastic horsemen. The Leader of the Opposition, the Hon. Norman Manley, was there.

I went into my stiff-handed, stiff-backed, tight-jawed mode, as I stood on the steps of the Premiere to greet our Minister and his wife, and other guests. Corina Meeks, Hartley Neita, Easton Lee and other staff helped to greet and usher people to their

"Time of Fury" Premiere

seats. We had mounted an exhibition on the work of the JIS in the foyer. Corina took the GG and other notables through it, before settling them in their seats. I don't think I could have managed very well without her that night.

The main members of the cast were called up on stage one by one, and the Minister introduced them to the audience: Sasso of the Water Commission, Aldridge (foreign language teacher at Calabar), Bobby Lee (actor and ex-RAF), Klause Merkens of Germany, Dennis Hall (Radio/TV personality and known actor), and all the others who sat among the audience (Jim Colby, Peter Hudson, Ilene Searle, Peggy Carley, Tony Wilson, Christopher Ball, George Madden, Henry Brash, Fitz Weir, Ronnie Harrison, Tony Henry, Cecil Cooper, Audley Coulton, Billy Dumont, Byron Dixon, Derek and Karl Dalhouse. Tribute was paid to Mapletoft Poulle, Ernest Ranglin and Errol Levy for recording the two original songs in the film.

During the showing I couldn't sit down. I was too tense and anxious; caught up again in every scene of the film. I stood by one of the exit doors. When it was all over and the guests were departing, I watched Norman Manley striding rapidly towards his car with a thoughtful, serious look on his face. I wondered what he was thinking. Our Minister seemed quite pleased. I felt like something that had been wrung dry.

Ten years later, in October 1975, when I was living in a kind of exile in "Outer Space," Michael Manley, who was then Prime Minister, wrote to me about "Time of Fury." He said:

> Dear Carey,
>
> I don't know if you are aware that your film "Time of Fury" was shown on JBC-TV last week as part of the many events put on for National Heritage week.
>
> I wanted you to know that a second viewing of this film re-confirmed my belief that it is an important

and moving work and a real contribution in Jamaica's continuing search to reconstruct our history from our own perspective.

I thought you might also like to know that many people to whom I spoke shared this view. I hope I can look forward to further works from you of the quality of "The Fighting Maroons" and "Time of Fury."

Warm and personal regards.

Michael Manley didn't sign the letter as Prime Minister, but just as Michael Manley; or more correctly (in his own handwriting) Michael. Reading his letter almost made my hair stand on end.

The amazing thing is that even though "Fury" had been made on a shoe-string, it had a very long life. Many years after the commemorative events of 1965 had been forgotten, "Fury" continued to be shown, in all its ragged dignity. Its' essential message never failed to strike home.

Visits

The Queen Mother visited Jamaica in February, 1965. As the person in charge of JIS, I got my first taste of introducing royalty to the press. The presentations were made in the ballroom at King's House. A large Superintendent of Police, Orville Bernard, hovered in the background. The Governor General, Sir Clifford Campbell, stood on the Queen Mother's left. I stood on her right. Some of my old Gleaner acquaintances were there. Theodore Sealy, Alva Ramsay (West Indian Sportsman), Barbara Gloudon, Clifton Neita, John Maxwell, (then editor of Public Opinion), H.P. Jacobs, Vere Johns, John Hearne, Stan Grant, Ray McKinley (PRO of the Ministry of Agriculture), Father John J. Sullivan (Catholic Opinion) Wyatt Bryce (PRO of the Jamaica Agricultural Society) and Aimee Webster of France Press. The trick was to remember all the names and organizations, and to keep cool. I had a distressing way of getting tense on such occasions.

One evening during the visit, the Queen Mother was getting ready to go to a reception. She was putting on her gloves in the room where we waited. There is a rule that royalty should not be photographed in the act of dressing. Our photographer (a freelancer) snapped the Queen Mother pulling on a glove. As the bulb flashed there was a general gasp of horror. A couple of aides leapt towards the photographer. I thought they were going to hurl him down the stairs. A stern demand was made for him to surrender the negative. Visibly shaken, the poor fellow fumbled the negative from his camera and handed it over, to be promptly destroyed.

Martin Luther King Jr., the famous U.S. civil rights activist and ardent advocate of passive (nonviolent) resistance, came to Jamaica in June 1965, to be the guest speaker at the graduation ceremony at the University of the West Indies. He couldn't help remarking on the feeling of freedom he personally experienced in Jamaica. Here, he did not have to face Jim Crow barriers of any sort. He didn't have to argue or demonstrate for tolerance. There was no question about his equal status as a human being. He went home to his native U.S. where he was assassinated in 1968.

The Queen's Visit

Her Majesty, Queen Elizabeth II, and his Royal Highness, the Duke of Edinburgh, re-visited Jamaica from March 3 to 6, 1966. The Queen's press secretary was Commander Sir Richard Colville K.C.V.O., C.B, D.S.C, R.N.; a rather stern-looking no-nonsense man. He was a stickler for detail and was going to make sure that everything went correctly and well, with strict observance of protocol. His job was to liaise with the press, largely through me. When I was introduced to him he looked me in the eye, and, with a very straight face, said: "Call me Sunshine."

On the first day of the visit, the Queen and the Duke, among other things, were scheduled to receive the press at King's House. I was to introduce the members of the press. Thank God I had some practice in 1965 when the Queen Mother visited. This was a grander affair, held in the large King's House drawing room. The Governor General brought in the Queen and the Duke and presented me to them. The press people were lined up and I began the presentations.

There was a feeling of good cheer and cordiality. It didn't matter whether you were a monarchist or the most way-out radical. The Queen was such a charming still-youthful woman, and the Duke looked so affable and dashing, that everyone just felt all right. After the introductions the press was organized into small groups around the room. I conducted the Queen from group to group for informal chats. Out of the corner of my eyes I could see

Sir Richard "Sunshine" Colville, watching my every move. "Above all," he had warned, "you must not touch the Queen." When it appeared to be time for her to move from one group to the next, I would continue to break into the conversation and tactfully indicate the next group.

The Queen seemed very relaxed, chatting amiably. I was very much taken with her warm approach. One of her shoes must have felt somewhat uncomfortable, for almost unconsciously she eased the foot partly out of the offending shoe, to give it a minor wriggle. She immediately rose to astronomical heights in my estimation. I was reminded of the incident in 1965 with the Queen Mother and her glove. There came an anxious moment, however, when it was time for the Queen to move on. She was so caught up in the conversation that she took no notice of my discreet efforts to intervene.

"Sunshine" hovered closer and made urgent signs, but the Queen, intent on making a vital point, seemed not to hear my voice. For one awful moment I raised my hand in desperation and almost touched her; but "Sunshine's" dread warning sounded in my ear: *Above all, you must not touch...*" so I had to raise my voice and finally got her to move. The day's activities ended with the Queen and the Duke meeting heads of the Diplomatic Missions at Kings House and "sitting" for photographs.

A fairly large crowd of specially invited guests had gathered in the grounds beneath the drawing room, for a reception. It was a glittering dressed-up affair. I took it into my head to stroll in splendid isolation along the roped-off route that would be used by the Queen and the Duke, on either side of which "the elite" were waiting. I still can't figure out why I did this, but nobody seemed to mind. Suddenly a messenger hurried up. I was wanted in the drawing room at once. I went up as fast as I could. The Queen and the Duke had finished their "sitting" for photographs and were about to descend to the lawn for the reception. "Sunshine" Colville, looking grim, informed me that no photographs were to be taken at the reception, and I was to please tell the press. No time to lose. You would have thought it was the end of the world.

The crowd outside had their eyes fixed on the drawing room doors. They were waiting for them to open and the Queen and Duke to emerge. Instead, when the doors opened, out burst Robinson, tearing down the long, wide steps at lightning speed, to warn off the photographers. A friend of mine, who was in the crowd, told me afterwards that he was highly amused by the whole thing.

Immediately after my rapid descent, the Queen and Duke (in contrast) came slowly and gracefully down the steps, escorted by the Governor General. Everything went off magnificently well. Not a single camera to be seen.

On the third day of the visit, a private dinner party was held on board the Royal Yacht Britannia, to which I was invited. Jamaican men attending the dinner party were instructed to wear tuxedos (black coats). The men in the Queen's party would wear white dinner jackets. I examined my bank account and decided I would either have to wear my white dinner jacket or turn down the invitation.

In defiance of instructions, I arrived at the Casa Blanca Pier (I believe that was the pier) resplendent in my white dinner jacket, to join the other guests who were awaiting the launch which would take us to the Britannia. I would be lying if I said I didn't feel like "the odd man." But that was a familiar status. I refused to imagine what my companions were thinking. As was to be expected, the dinner was magnificent.

At the end of it the Queen and the Duke retired to a small compartment, where they received each of the guests, and handed out gifts. Major Trevor Robinson had been the Jamaican Equerry to the royal party from the start. He stood nearby as guests were received. When my turn came the Queen asked if he was related to me.

"No, ma'm," I said, *"he's no kin of mine."* The Queen said that she understood I had some trouble at one time in the tour. All I could think of was "Sunshine" Colville's last-minute "request" to ban the photographers during the reception. I said something about it all being "grist to the mill," for I was feeling somewhat light-tongued after so many fine glasses of wine. The Queen then presented me with my gift: a gold pen and pencil set.

Emperor Haile Selassie's Visit

On April 21, 1966, only about a month and a half after the Queen's visit, His Imperial Majesty Haile Selassie I of Ethiopia, came to Jamaica. Inevitably, the nature of the visit was vastly different.

Haile Selassie (otherwise known as Ras Tafari) had had a difficult time. He came to the throne of Ethiopia in 1930. Five years later the Italians invaded the country and took over. Selassie was forced to flee. In 1941, during World War II, he was able to regain the throne and get rid of the Italians with the aid of Britain and the Commonwealth. In December 1960, nearly six years before he came to Jamaica, he was on a state visit to Brazil when there was an attempted coup by dissidents in Ethiopia. It was suppressed after three days by loyal supporters, and the Emperor hurried back home.

In Jamaica, the Rastafari religion which centered on Emperor Selassie had been growing for many years. The Government knew they would have to deal with the Rastafarians when the Emperor visited, but they did not anticipate the power of emotion that would be let loose. It was not going to be business as usual.

The JIS Film Unit was at the Palisadoes Airport (now Norman Manley) to record the Emperor's arrival. I was scheduled to introduce the press to the Emperor at King's House. I drove to the airport to witness the start of this most historic visit. On the way I saw many Rastafarians crowded into vehicles or hurrying along on foot. As I drew closer to the airport the number increased, all moving rapidly, with intense expressions on their faces.

When I arrived at the airport I went on to the tarmac, where the Emperor would be received by the Governor General, Sir Clifford Campbell, and the acting Prime Minister, the Hon. Donald Sangster. The areas reserved for spectators were filling up rapidly, mostly with Rastafarians.

The red-coated Guard of Honour was out on the tarmac. There was a platform with a microphone. The VIPs were arriving: Cabinet Ministers, some Senators, the Attorney General, the Chief Justice, the Speaker of the House, the acting President of the Court of Appeal, the Dean of the Diplomatic Corps, Hon. N.W. Manley, Leader of the Opposition; eminent churchmen (Bishop Gibson, Bishop John McEleney, Rev. Hugh Sherlock) and others. Police were all about.

The Emperor's plane appeared in the sky, and a cry went up from the dense ranks of Rastafarians. The acting Prime Minister gazed uneasily at them. The JIS cameramen, Franklyn (Chappie) St. Juste, took a shot of the Guard of Honor, then turned his camera on the incoming plane. The plane landed and began to taxi towards the place where the welcoming ceremony would be held. St. Juste turned again to get a shot of the crowd. Just then the Rastafarians gave a great shout and surged forward. Their Emperor had arrived. They would not be relegated to "holding areas." They had to get up close; perhaps close enough to be able to touch the object of their adoration. St. Juste was engulfed in the roaring tide of Rastafarians. They swept him away, towards the plane. He had to hold his camera over his head to protect it. The police were pushed aside. The Rastas ran through the ranks of soldiers and leapt across the platform, almost knocking down the acting Prime Minister and the astonished VIPs.

It is difficult to tell what happened next. The portable steps had somehow reached the door of the plane. The door was opened.

Security personnel were around the steps. Major Trevor Robinson, who had been the Jamaican Equerry to the Queen during her visit, was on the steps. The shouting Rastas were almost at the plane-side. The Emperor came forward in full uniform, and stood in the doorway. He looked at the sea of bearded faces staring up at him and raised his arms to quiet them. But they shouted all the more, perhaps mis-reading his gestures. It was an impossible situation. All order had disappeared. The Emperor stepped backwards and vanished into the plane.

Apart from the jubilant Rastafarians everyone was in shock. The whole thing had happened so suddenly and quickly. Someone wisely got hold of one of the foremost Rastafarian leaders; I think it was Mortimo Planno. He was ushered onto the plane and spent a long time inside. He came back out on to the steps. I believe Trevor Robinson or someone else gave him a bullhorn. He asked for calm, and appealed to the crowd to move back from the side of the plane so that the Emperor could come out. I had lost all track of time, and cannot tell how long it was before the situation was brought under control, and the Emperor was able to leave the plane. St. Juste thought it was about an hour.

Anyway, the Emperor finally came out, acknow-ledged the acclamation of the large crowd, got into one of the waiting cars which had come on to the tarmac, and was taken away. I was told later that some Rastafarians thought it was not the Emperor but a substitute. They had expected a much bigger man. His majestic photographs and the great reverence in which he was held, had led them to assume that he was of "heroic" stature.

There had, of course, been no welcoming ceremony. The whole occasion melted away into an indescribable atmosphere of post-exaltation wonder. I picked my way drunkenly through the turmoil, almost forgetting that I had to be at King's House to present the press to the Emperor. His Imperial Majesty had been taken to the National Stadium for another ceremony. I thought that would give me plenty of time to get to King's House before he arrived there. I hurried to my car; but by then it was almost too late. Traffic had already built up on the Palisadoes Road; all kinds of vehicles. I tried to overtake vehicles ahead of me, but the line was endless. Soon it was going at a snail's pace. I began to get anxious. I had on my jacket and it was hot. Ancient vehicles broke down here and there, and blocked the road. Driving in low gear with the frequent need to stop was a strain on engines. Cars began to overheat. My own engine began to boil. Somewhere along the way I stopped, to cool the engine and to get some water to pour into the radiator. Then back into the line. The minutes flew by as I crawled along. Surely the ceremony at the National Stadium must be over by now, and the Emperor on his way to King's House. I was almost overcome by frustration.

My suit was damp and rumpled; my face sweaty. Despair began to set in. I was going to miss this once-in-a-life-time opportunity. By the time I cleared Windward Road, the traffic began to thin out. Late or not I had to make an effort. I drove as fast as I could. Hindsight took hold of me. What I should have done in the first place was go behind the line of cars escorting the Emperor. Out-riders had been in front with their sirens, clearing the way. Instead I lingered at the airport, bemused by what had happened. I prayed that the Emperor had been delayed at the stadium.

When I raced through the gates of King's House I could tell from the look of things that the Emperor had already arrived. Cars and security people were all over the place. I parked in the first available space and ran towards the house. In my crushed and sweat-stained suit my appearance was anything but fresh. I flew through the entrance and leapt up the broad stairs towards the drawing rooms. The Emperor was standing inside the room facing the doorway. The Governor General was standing at his right, and Major Trevor Robinson was at his left. Since I had not appeared, Trevor had been put beside the Emperor to substitute for me. Standing beside Trevor was Ken Chaplin, Senior Information Officer in the JIS Press section, who had apparently been drafted to assist Trevor with the names of members of the press who were to be presented. As soon as I burst upon the scene Trevor immediately stepped aside. The Governor General introduced me to the Emperor and I took my place at his left. The introductions began. The Emperor was dignified, formal, even grave. He did not have the smiling, almost cheerful demeanor of the Queen Mother, the Queen or the Duke of Edinburgh. But he seemed to convey a controlled respect for each person whose hand he shook. He was small and almost delicately-made, but he stood very straight and had a "manly" presence.

His commanding countenance and large steady eyes made you forget his lack of size. I seem to recall that he had a small dog somewhere near him. I felt most fortunate that I had been able to reach King's House in the nick of time.

While in Kingston the Emperor addressed both Houses of Parliament, received an honorary degree of Doctor of Law at the University of the West Indies at a special ceremony, toured the Payne Avenue Project and had a school named after him. The Government had wisely arranged for the Emperor to meet and talk with the top Rastafarian leaders, and this greatly helped to give them a sense of inclusion in the visit. But the mass of Rastafarians were far from satisfied. They still wanted to be in his presence. They wanted him in their midst.

The Emperor left Kingston by train for Spanish Town where a ceremony was to be held. When the train arrived at the Spanish Town station where the VIP's had gathered, a huge crowd of Rastafarians were present. A Police Superintendent advised the authorities not to let the Emperor leave the train. When the

Rastafarians learned that the Emperor was not getting off they were outraged. They hurled aside the chairs which had been placed to accommodate the VIP's and stormed the train, determined to be in the presence of their Emperor. Once again, JIS cameraman Franklin St. Juste was on the spot to capture whatever action he could. Mostly what he caught was up turned chairs, clouds of rising dust, and a one-legged man hopping amid the chaos. The train got away with some difficulty. At the Montego Bay Airport on the Emperor's departure, stout rope barriers were erected to hold back the crowd. The scene, though lively, was more controlled. Indeed, there was a note of sadness. The Rastafarians stood reverently and sang hymns, as their beloved Emperor went away and left them. I don't think Jamaica had ever seen such an out-pouring of emotion.

Germany

In September 1966, about five months after Emperor Selassie's visit, my mother died. She had been a sort of Amazon; a warrior woman. But she had a gift of turning a house into a warm and wonderful home, and she had a tremendous influence on all the young people who came into her sphere. Shortly before her death, the German Ambassador in Jamaica, Dr. Phillip Schmidt-Schlegel, invited me to visit Germany.

Dr. Schmidt-Schlegel was tall, robust and black haired. He had a forthright, ardent manner and told me he had been a soldier in the German Army on the Russian front in World War II. The member of the German embassy who saw me off at the airport was Dr. Eitel who was tall, blond, erect, and strenuous in appearance. As a boy, he had been a member of the Hitler Youth, and he remembered those days with a certain nostalgia.

The Hitler Youth organization had given him a feeling of high aspiration, commitment and purpose. I remember my own naïve fascination with the iron-faced, jack-booted enemy of World War II, even though I knew what would have happened to people like myself if they had won.

We flew from Kingston to Montego Bay, where we got off for a short stop. Just when we were getting ready to board, a rumour reached the airport that there was a bomb on the plane. We waited while every piece of luggage was searched and the plane was given a thorough "going over". After about an hour and a half, it was announced that no bomb had been found. We boarded to begin the first leg of the flight which would take us to New York. Two passengers cancelled their flight arrangements and a man was ejected for having the "wrong" ticket. As we took off I had to suppress the thought of the plane exploding in mid air. At New York we got off and waited forty-five minutes, then were told to board again.

As we took our seats we were told to get off. We were taken in buses to a nearby hotel to spend the night while the plane was again searched. We finally took off in the morning, bound for Frankfurt. I was travelling First Class. My only companion was a very tall man probably in his mid-fifties with a severe countenance. We spoke not a word to each other during the journey.

The plane arrived at Frankfurt several hours late because of the delay in New York. After all the delays and searches, my luggage could not be found. Mrs. Haffke the official, who met me, looked high and low, but no success. While we were going up and down we passed my only "cabin companion" from the plane. We both bowed to each other and mumbled a greeting. Over come by curiosity I asked Mrs. Haffke who he was. She told me he was an eminent museum official who had recently lost his son in a helicopter crash somewhere in Africa.

I took the plane for Cologne (Ko'In-Bonn) with what I stood in and carried in my hand. On arrival I was met by Jurgen Klaus, who was to be my guide. He took me to Bonn, the seat of the Federal Government. I stayed in a hotel which was built on the site of a ruined medieval castle. I found Bonn to be small, clean and pretty. The only statue in the town was one of Beethoven, who was born there. My luggage didn't arrive that night or the next day. So I went to a store and bought socks, a shirt, and other personal necessities. The sales clerk had to measure my neck for the shirt. When I tried it on in the hotel the neck was too tight. I took it back. I leaned forward as I had done before, and she measured again. "See," she said, "it is correct." But the neck was still too tight. That night my luggage arrived.

I went to the Federal Parliament. The chamber was big and high, with a huge figure of a German eagle on one wall. Chancellor Erhard and the other Parliamentarians were in a heated debate over a plane called the Star-fighter. I had lunch at a sidewalk restaurant at the edge of a busy road. Everything was very orderly. No hassle or loud noises. I thought how wonderful it would be if that could happen in Kingston.

The next day I was invited to lunch at the Press Club Centre, and had an interesting conversation with my hosts about the German Army. Dr. Hubener of the Foreign Department, who was a keen student of Military history, spoke with great fervor. I was rewarded for my interest when Dr. Hubener presented me with a book called "Jackboot, the Story of the German soldier." It was written by John Laffin who had visited over one hundred battlefields on which German or Prussian soldiers had fought. After two days I left at night for Hamburg, where I was met at the airport by my new guide; a brilliant young man named Peter Heim. All my guides spoke excellent English. Peter Heim also spoke Spanish and French. He was an ex-army lieutenant who seemed to know everything, and was extremely efficient.

Hamburg is a city with a tremendous port; at the time it was said to be the fifth largest in the world. The most interesting person I met was Dr. Schultz-Kamphfhenkel, a famous maker of documentary films. Peter Heim and I had dinner with him, then went to his home and looked at some of his films. His home was unpretentious but full of interesting things. I thoroughly enjoyed the evening and got back to the hotel at 1:10am.

The next day I took a one-hour ferry ride around the crowded harbour (the Port of Hamburg) with its cold, grey water and ships of all nations. Like Bonn, Hamburg had many green parks with trees. What a "civilizing" difference they made. Flowers were everywhere, in beds or large concrete pots. The biggest thrill of all, however, was when Peter Heim took me to see the colossal statue of Otto Von Bismarck, unifier of Germany, first Chancellor of the German Empire (the iron Chancellor). I stood near the Press Centre. I had never seen anything so grim, brooding, powerful and awe-inspiring. I got a telephone call from a film-maker named Werner Grassman. He had been in Jamaica some time before and I had given him some assistance. He had seen a story in one of the newspapers about my visit to Hamburg, and invited me to have supper with him. It was a meal mostly of wine, cheese and very good buttered bread, served on wooden platters. Somehow, it seemed like one of the best meals I ever had. The unpretentious home of Werner Grassman and Dr. Schuz-Kampfhenkel really impressed me. There was something about them that seemed straight-forward and solid. With no need to impress. I left Hamburg on Sunday morning for Berlin. On the way to the airport, Peter Heim brought his girlfriend along in a car to "look at me" I guess. At Berlin Airport I was met by a new guide, Werner Neuhaus. He had one arm, having lost the other in an accident three years before. As a result, he was always cautioning the driver of our car not to speed too much.

As soon as I checked in at the hotel, the Ambassador for Berlin took me to see the Berlin Wall. We looked at it from about three or four different points, and it was really ghastly. All along the wall, wherever people had been killed trying to get across, there were terrible-looking dried-up wreathes with the names of the slain. On either side of the wall the land was devastated and the houses empty and dilapidated, it looked worst on the Eastern side. We climbed up on look-out points along with other sightseers, and gazed into East Berlin. In addition to the wall there were iron barriers and barbed-wire fences to prevent vehicles from breaking through. East-German soldiers could be seen through the fence peering at the sight-seers through binoculars. At the check-points on the West side, the German guards were armed with sub-machine guns. I also saw French, American and British soldiers.

After we left the wall we drove around to West Berlin. I saw the ruined Reichstag (the former Legislative Assembly building of Germany), the Victory Monument (built to commemorate the 1870 war against the French) and a monument to fallen Russian soldiers, guarded by two young Russian officers armed with sub-machine guns. The Russian monument was actually in West Berlin, and it was funny to see the Russian officers grinning and waving at the bus-loads of tourists, who were also grinning and waving at them.

Werner Neuhaus took me to the tomb of the men who had plotted to kill Hitler with a bomb, and who had been hanged (or rather strangled). Their bodies had been burnt and the ashes scattered to the wind. Part of the prison where they were killed forms the monument to them.

On September 26, I went over into East Berlin. I was driven and escorted by an Arab (Syrian) student named Yassin Tarabishi. My regular guide (Werner Neuhaus) wasn't allowed to go, as he was a West Berliner and they were not permitted to go over. We showed our passports to the West Berlin guard, then drove cautiously across the stretch of "no man's land." A big, blond East German guard (who would have delighted Hitler's heart) let us through the gate. We were told to get out of the car which was then thoroughly searched: trunk, inside and bonnet.

A guard looked searchingly at our passports. We were sent into a room where the passports were again examined. They seemed to be having some trouble with my green official Jamaican passport. Perhaps they had never seen one like it. I allowed my mind the luxury of imagining that I would be detained and interrogated under torture by some Gestapo Survivor. Finally my passport was returned and my guide and I were given forms to fill out. After that we were obligated to convert five marks into the equivalent of East German money. We were then allowed to get into our car and drive to another gate. There our passports were again scrutinized before we were allowed to proceed into the East German gate.

For a few blocks adjacent to the wall on the Eastern side, the place looked like a ghost town. Beyond that, as far as I could see, East Berlin appeared grim, untidy and unrepaired. Lots of war damage was still present. The Arab guide, Yassin Tarabishi, took me to a magnificent museum, the Staaliche Museum Zu Berlin Antiken Sammlung. It contained artifacts and architectural remains from ancient Persia, Assyria, and Roman places. I was vastly impressed. The museum building was surrounded by a moat.

We went to a big park in a forest to see a war monument for five thousand Russian soldiers who had been buried there. It was a tremendous monument, well cared for, well-ordered, ghostly-grim, reflecting agony and sacrifice. Yassin Tarabishi and I bought big sausages and slices of bread with mustard at the Russian monument. I wanted to go back to see the rest of the museum but there wasn't time. As we went back to the gates I noticed that two areas stood out among the dilapidated looking scene. They were the Karl Marx Alley which was beautifully laid-out, and the Unter Den Linden Avenue, with its central promenade lined with Linden trees.

At the gates we had to go through the same passport and search procedure. They made sure we had spent the five marks we had converted into East German money. I left Berlin for Munich (M'UNCHEN). The city is the capital of the state of Bavaria, which is the most "beer-drinkingest state in the whole of beer drinking Germany". When I arrived it was in the throes of the October-fest, an annual festival at which Bavarians drink more beer.

The theory was that beer soothes the nerves and calms the disposition. Peter Reichel boasted that everything in Bavria was free and independent, including the happy cows. He told me with pride that their greatest King was Ludwig, who, among other things, had twenty-four mistresses, apparently all at the same time. One of these mistresses, Lola Montez, eventually caused him to abdicate his throne. We went to a crowded beer hall and drank beer out of one litre stone mugs. Men, women and teenagers were drinking beer. I saw wagons loaded with casks of beer being pulled by giant horses. I also saw someone who, in my romantic imaginations looked like a product of the post-war military occupation. Amid all those blond or very fair-skinned people, a brown girl appeared. She wore a mini skirt and was about sixteen or seventeen. Her hair was not straight but was combed out. She looked healthy and attractive. For some reason I felt enormously sorry for her, although I was sure there was no need for that. I had seen foreign students in the cities I passed through: Africans, Japanese and Syrians. I had also seen Italian workers. But this girl looked like a product of the place. I left Munich on Thursday, September 29, bound for Stuttgart. I was somewhat sorry to part with my "free and independent" student guide, Peter Reichel, whose comic character had given a merry note to my trip.

I took the train to Stuttgart. It was a brief visit. My main point of interest was an organization devoted to keeping in touch with German communities all over the world. I think it was called the Institut f'ur Auslandsbeziehungen. It sent out books, exhibitions, etc... to keep German nationals up-to-date on the latest cultural happenings in Germany. It also collected books, pamphlets, slides and pictures from the countries where German expatriate communities were located, and from countries with which it had established cultural ties.

After a quick tour of Stuttgart, I boarded the train for Frankfurt. I was sitting alone in a small compartment when a man appeared in the doorway. He was tall and broad and was wearing a hat and a trench-coat. He stood there for a little while, looking at me as if I was some unwelcome intruder. He seemed to be trying to make up his mind. Then suddenly he smiled, and took a seat. I arrived at Frankfurt about three in the afternoon. The usual guide wasn't there to meet me. I stood where I could be easily seen, and waited. After a while a tall young man wearing a sports jacket hurried up. He introduced himself: Klaus Herman; and apologized for being a bit late. There was a traffic jam on the road, caused by an accident. But, accident or not, I soon found out that Klaus had a punctuality problem. He was also a "radical."

Klaus had unruly brown hair. He was twenty-eight and had been thrown out of a university, along with a bunch of other radical students, for expressing unacceptable radical views. I wondered what those views were. He was a sociology student and was currently writing his master's thesis at the University of Frankfurt. He confessed that he had been up until six o'clock that morning with a girlfriend. She was an actress and was soon to be married (to someone else). I thought that was probably the real reason he came late to the train station. Everything had to be crammed into that day, as I was scheduled to leave Germany in the morning. Among other things we went to the home of Goethe, the German poet, dramatist, novelist and scientist; the creator of the dramatic poem "Faust" in which he said: *"He alone deserves freedom as well as life, who has to win them by conquest every day."*

We stopped at Klaus Hermann's home. He lived in a basement which he furnished with old furniture and an odd assortment of stringed instruments.

The next morning there was a fog all over the city. I was told it was a typical autumn day. It was the day of my departure from Germany, and Klaus Hermann was again late. The plane also took off late.

My visit to Germany, coming right after the death of my mother, had an uneasy effect on me. I began to feel more intensely, the absence in my country, of the "evidence" of its passage through time, and of the exertions of the "best" of its people.

The Fractured Giant

In 1966, JBC's Chairman, K.H. Ivan Levy, tried to get me to join the Corporation to take charge of its Programmes Department. By that time, JIS Radio and TV were well established in the public mind as a popular and credible force in the electronic media. In contrast, the "giant" Corporation, which occupied an enviable place of importance as the national station, was weakened by internal frictions. The Engineering section, headed by Laurie Stewart (who was made Chief Engineer in 1965) was well run. There were serious individuals in the Programmes Department and in News who had a professional approach. But despite praiseworthy efforts here and there, nothing was really taking off. Some five general managers had appeared and disappeared in the space of about seven years. Mickey Hendricks had stayed the longest, about three years. Harvey Ennevor, who succeeded him, lasted only about a year. Now Merrick Needham was about to act as general manger.

This was the scene that Ivan Levy wanted me to enter. The thought of going into that pool of quicksand made my heart sink. What chance would I have to "do my own thing?" On October 6, 1966, shortly after my return from Germany, I wrote Ivan saying that the last few years had "spoiled" me for anything but the "command post". For all practical purposes my only "boss" had been the Minister, who, subject to the proper execution of my duties, had left me a pretty free hand. I would therefore find it difficult to accept this offer. The rehabilitation of JBC would require a lot of imagination and bold thinking: the dismantling and replacement of a lot of things which had accumulated in the administrative ruins left by successive general managers. I could only accept the challenge if I had the freedom (under the Board) to stand or fall by my own decisions. I thought that would be the end of the matter, but the Minister summoned me. We had a long chat one evening about the need to "learn the ropes" before taking up the post of manager. I told him I would think it over and come back o him.

Several weeks later I wrote the Minister and told him that my general approach was not in line with the present system at JBC, and it would be folly to subject myself to it. I knew there was a lot to learn. That was not the problem. There was a need for an inspired approach, and that was not something one could "learn."

When I got that off my chest I honestly hoped it would be the end of the matter. But I have since come to feel that the Almighty has his own agenda for each of us. And looking back now, I think that what finally happened was directly responsible for the arrival of my five granddaughters. But to be honest, I must confess that I was "mildly" insulted that anyone should think of asking me to exchange my chair at JIS, for a subordinate seat in a fractured situation, whose way-of-life would surely destroy me. The Corporation gave me the feeling of a ship without a rudder, moving aimlessly through the water.

Busta Steps Down

1967 was a momentous year in the political life of Jamaica. The first General Elections since Independence were held on February 21. The JLP won thirty-three seats to the PNP's twenty. Around that time, Bustamante, who was still Prime Minister, officially retired. He was eighty-three. He had been around for about thirty years, dominating the labour scene and much of the political life. He was now a rather grandfatherly figure. Still, I could hardly imagine the political life of Jamaica without him.

There had been rumours of a struggle within the JLP for leadership. Donald Sangsters and Robert Lightbourne appeared to be the top contenders. But there were others, including Clem Tavares and Hugh Shearer. Lightbourne was articulate, confident and carried himself like a patrician. He felt he was close to Busta because he had supported "the Chief" in his stand on Federation. Now he was rivaling Donald Sangster for the top post. But there was still only one bull in the JLP pen, and that was Busta. He wanted Donald Sangster to be Prime Minister and there could be no argument. No one fooled with Busta. Nobody in his party really wanted to fight him. In Busta's presence, Donald Sangster, like all his colleagues, was deferential.

I recall looking at the television on the night of the victory celebrations following the JLP win in 1967. The cameras were trained on the celebrating crowd at Jamaica House. Baz Freckleton (who had been a sports reporter at the Gleaner while I was there, but was now in the JBC Newsroom) was standing in front of a camera like a wooden statue, with a microphone in his hand. He was trying to say something, trying to get Mr. Sangster to speak; but was pushed around by the press of bodies and in danger of being knocked off his feet. His face became more and more wooden as the camera continued to be trained relentlessly on him. His eyes took on a glassy look. It was almost a fiasco. I felt relieved when Mr. Sangster finally managed to struggle to the microphone, to address the waiting nation. Donald Burns Sangster was sworn in as Prime Minister by Governor General, Sir Clifford Campbell, on February 23, 1967: the second Prime Minister of Independent Jamaica. He worked very hard, in a sort of "pressure-cooker" environment. A JIS film shot in Parliament caught him shifting uneasily in his chair; looking tired and unwell. A little over three weeks after being sworn in as Prime Minister, he was struck down by a brain haemorrhage. The nation was stunned. Mr. Sangster was flown to Montreal for emergency treatment. People who saw him being put on the plane thought he was dead. Rumours began to fly around immediately about in-fighting in the JLP camp for leadership.

Clem Tavares was a very ambitious man, but he was ailing. Bob Lightbourne looked lean and hard and was ready to take the prize. Hugh Shearer was an enigma; tall and likable; and everybody knew that Busta regarded him almost as a son. Which one would be the next Prime Minister?

It didn't seem like Mr. Sangster would recover. The JLP didn't have much time. A vote was taken at a hastily called party conference to determine who should succeed Donald Sangster. It appeared that Clem Tavares was out in front, followed closely by Hugh Shearer with Bob Lightbourne third. But the long arm of Bustamante reached out to take control of the situation. That first vote was a preliminary. Let's go now for the "real thing." In the second contest it was said that Hugh Shearer won by one vote, over Clem Tavares. In the meantime, Mr. Sangster was in the Montreal Neurological Institute, seemingly in a coma. The British Government knighted him "by proxy" as he lay on his death bed. When he died on April 11, he was Sir Donald Sangster, Knight Commander of the Royal Victorian Order. He was fifty-five years old.

Four hours after his death, the news reached Jamaica. Hugh Lawson Shearer was sworn in by the Governor General, Sir Clifford Campbell, as the third Prime Minister of the country. Sir Donald's body was flown to Jamaica and taken by train to lie in State at Mountainside (his home community), Chapelton and then Kingston. JIS did a TV/Radio programme on his life and death, the State funeral and the burial at the George VI Memorial Park (now National Heroes Park). Early the next year (1968) the ailing Clem Tavares died. He was just forty-three.

In September, 1967, shortly after Sir Donald Sangster's death, I was confirmed in the post as head of JIS. I was finally off "the edge of the knife." During the period I was "acting" nobody who was honest could deny the constructive and highly creative work we did in documenting the country's history. Our achievements, reliability and trustworthiness far outweighed the few times when we may have stumbled.

The long period of acting would have been demoralizing if I had not been caught up in all the challenges.

A Distressing Moment

Spurred by what I felt was the emptiness of our "roots landscape", I started to research and write more than ever. My manuscript got very large. I was advised to cut, cut and cut. I finally decided that instead of trying to do one massive work, I would lift out the story of the Maroons. I worked at night, after I got home from the office and on weekends.

In the midst of this exercise, K.H. Ivan Levy, Chairman of the JBC Board, re-opened the subject of my going over to the Corporation, this time as general manager. It made my hair stand on end. I had seen too much of the raw, naked insides of the Corporation; all the cracks and fractures. I had been a front-row, "ringside" witness to the futile struggles of general managers. I thought the only way to save myself was to take off the gloves and hit-out hard with what was in my heart; settle this business once and for all.

I wrote the Minister on July 17, 1968, saying that Mr. Levy had offered me the job of general manager, and thought it was necessary to make my position quite clear. I said I had participated in and observed the Broadcasting scene in Jamaica for sixteen years. I had sat on the JBC Board for six of those years. In my estimation the post of general manager had lost status and power. Ever since the strike its prestige and prerogatives had been steadily whittled away. At the present moment it seemed nothing more than a glorified messenger boy for the Board. Every fledging board member, within a few weeks of arrival, considered himself or herself obliged to instruct the GM about everything under the sun, particularly what his or her acquaintances liked or disliked. The GM was too much at the mercy of the Board. The organization could not flourish unless the professional status of the manager was recognized. Broadcasting was a specialized field, and not a thing of whim and fancy.

As a first step I strongly recommended that the post of GM be upgraded to Managing Director. I stuck my neck out further by saying that in order to develop confidence in the integrity of JBC, the nation (through Government) would have to be assured that the station would not become a political tool, or a platform for cranks and sinister people. The Corporation must be allowed to reflect, in a constructive manner, the important issues of national life, with a view to the orderly and reasonable development of the Jamaican society.

It would not be worthwhile for me to take up this potentially important post if the present job conditions were allowed to continue. Having been so outspoken, I didn't think it would be fair to Ivan Levy if I didn't let him know what I said to the Minister; so I sent him a copy of the letter.

Ivan Levy was deeply wounded and outraged. He wrote to inform me that he was calling an emergency board meeting. To this day I cannot read his reply without a feeling of distress, for I really liked the man. I admired his courage, loyalty and determination to stand by his beliefs, even if I didn't share some of them. At my written request he cancelled the emergency meeting. Once he cooled down I think he appreciated my honest approach; although to tell you the truth, I had expected some kind of savage reprisal. But, as it turned out, I was soon able to feel at ease in the boardroom once more. In my letter to him which caused him to cancel the emergency meeting, I said:

I have valued our association over the past six years. I remember very well (my) first board meeting, how you greeted me warmly, which immediately put me at ease, and tried to draw me into the proceedings at the earliest opportunity. I have learnt a lot from observing your methods as Chairman and I have come to admire your nerve and courage, especially during moments of crisis. I have never really seen you lose heart even when the going was tough, and I believe you have tried to be fair to everyone. Naturally I have not always agreed with you, and very often I have refrained from speaking my mind when perhaps I should have.

I am happy that you have thought sufficiently well of me to ask me, two or three times, to go to work with JBC, and in a sense, I think I have let you down each time not because of the Board or anything else, but because my own character and personality would not allow me to fit comfortably into the scheme of things as they exist.

I would... like to go on record as saying that I believe JBC Radio has improved a great deal.... The news presentation is excellent and the production techniques are of a high standard. I am confident that the organization will keep on surmounting the obstacles with which it is faced.

I wasn't buttering up Ivan Levy when I wrote that letter. It was what I believed, and how I felt. But I fervently hoped that the subject of my going over to JBC would never come up again.

Norman Manley Goes Away

When Sir Donald Sangster died in 1967 (after less than fifty days as Prime Minister), Norman Manley was interviewed in the front yard of JBC. It was a filmed interview. I don't exactly remember his words now, but he said something like this: "*Sometimes life gives some hard and cruel blows...*" He said those words with passion; almost with bitterness; and it seemed to me he was talking about himself, rather than about Sir Donald Sangster.

To me, Norman Manley's life was like a Greek tragedy. He reminded me also of a medieval knight in rusting armour, with a shining sword, emerging from a broken-down castle in a dark ruined countryside. In this derelict landscape, he was a sort of aristocrat among the small farmers and labourers. And even when he was walking through the bush with his rough companions looking for cattle, or chipping logwood with an axe, there was in him a special feeling. Later in his life, he dismissed his heritage in a few terse sentences. He never seemed driven to dig deeper than the immediate Shearers on his mother's side, or his Yorkshire paternal grandfather. His father died when he was only a boy. In a sense, Norman Manley seemed to embody his ancestral lines within the ambit of his own being, without the need for tracing.

When he rode furiously on his horse from school at Beckford and Smith, through Spanish Town towards his home at Belmont, and was held by the police for recklessness, he was just a young patrician expressing his natural self. When he went to Jamaica College (an enclave of privilege in those days) and found himself among young lordlings, he used his fists and force of his spirit to make himself their master. For he had been physically and mentally toughened by his strenuous boyhood in the country.

He was saved from a path of irresponsible arrogance by the death of his mother when he was about sixteen. It shook him up. He stopped being a rough-house tough-guy and became a serious student. And here again he out-classed the young lordlings of his generation by winning the Rhodes Scholarship, the gateway to the stronghold of the Pukka Sahibs, bequeathed by the arch imperialist, Cecil Rhodes. His encounter with raw racial prejudice in the British Army during World War I, the death of his beloved brother in battle, and his front line participation in the bloody, muddy battle of the Somme, stripped him of the fanciful foolishness which made the Jamaican ruling class an almost useless bunch where the welfare of the people was concerned. His marriage to his cousin Edna, was another daring event in the tapestry of his extraordinary life. And the revelation that his arch rival, the irrepressible Alexander Bustamante, was his cousin, was another intriguing thing on his escutcheon. Busta had worked on Manley's mother's derelict Belmont property as a junior overseer for about a year, before going off on his overseas adventures. Norman Manley had played dominoes with him, and watched him tame wild horses. He was only about nine years old at the time, to Busta's nineteen or so. All of it was story-book material.

When Norman Manley crowned his unusual career by becoming what many thought to be the foremost barrister in Jamaica, he seemed to enter a throne room for which he had been destined. But there, instead of enriching himself, or placing his feet complacently upon the backs of the people, he had given up his bright legal career to go into the grim, newly-built arena of Jamaican partisan politics.

He had put all the considerable force of his intellect and will into the political process, driven by a vision of what Jamaica might become for a neglected and largely dispossessed people. But he had to watch his cousin Bustamante take Jamaica into the promised land of Independence, which he himself had struggled so hard to achieve. Now his health seemed ruined, his strength draining away, as he contemplated the unsatisfactory end of his personal endeavours.

He consented to do a filmed interview with the JIS. I wanted to interview him myself, but he seemed to be in such a sharp, impatient mood that I asked Corina Meeks to do it, thinking he might relax more with a woman asking the questions. Half way through the interview the film reel ran out. Mr. Manley had to pause in mid-sentence while a fresh reel was put into the camera (Clive Grannum) asked him to repeat his last sentence. Mr. Manley almost leapt out of his chair. "I'm not repeating anything" he said angrily. I thought he was going to leave but we managed to diffuse the tense moment and the interview continued.

In February, 1969, Norman Manley resigned as Leader of the Opposition and as a member of the House of Representatives. His second son, Michael, was elected as leader of the party, and became Leader of the Opposition. It was over for Norman Manley. He, who could have been a wealthy man, was on the verge of financial ruin. His home "Drumblair," which had been his landed domain, had been sold, to help meet financial demands. He didn't even seem to have the desire to complete his memoirs, to the great loss of the country. It was said that he was offered a knight-hood, but refused it. We heard he was not at all well, and had taken to bed. But I vaguely thought he would get back on his feet. Then one day, Frank Hill, the political commentator, phoned me to say that Norman Manley was dying. He was almost gone. Perhaps JIS should start to gather material for the evening TV programme. We got together all the films and photographs we could find or borrow, and I started to write a script. In the midst of everything, word came that Norman Manley was dead. That evening I went on the JIS programme with a half-finished script, and partly ad-libbed my way through the half hour. Our TV production staff did a great job. We were there, on time, giving Jamaica something in-depth to think about. Norman Manley died on September 2, 1969, about seven months after he retired. I went to Heroes' Park when the grave was being prepared. Norman Manley's granddaughter, Rachel, came up and introduced herself, petite and unassuming. Watching the Manley family, shrouded in mourning-black on the day of the funeral, was devastating; especially the widow, Edna Manley. The new Prime Minister, Hugh Shearer was at the grave side. The closest I came to understanding Norman Manley, was through something he said in the interview with Corina Meeks.

Corina asked:- *"Is there nothing at all in your career as a barrister that you would like to record, nothing that sticks out in your mind?"*

N.W. Manley: *"Hard work, seven days a week, sixteen to eighteen hours a day. That's what sticks out in my mind."*

Corina: *"Would you attribute your success as a barrister to pure research or was it your flair for courtroom work, or was it a combination of both?"*

N.W. Manley: *"It was hard work first of all. It was absolutely egotistic determination to win every case I was engaged in, which I regard as the most important attribute of an advocate. A famous judge was once asked by a father: 'What advice can you give me to give my son now that he proposes to go into the bar?'"*

And he replied: *"Sir, remind the young man that he must have high animal spirits; that is the first requirement. And the second is the same, and the third is the same. And if, in addition, the young gentleman did learn a little law, he won't do too badly."*

In other words, just a capacity for hard work and a total will to win; so that you stop at nothing. Maximum concentration, maximum personal observation, maximum study, maximum everything. And the reward was winning.

Norman Manley relied too much on his own considerable personal strength. And being human, his personal strength was finite.

England

On September 8, 1969, six days after Norman Manley died, Jamaica officially changed its money from the traditional pounds, shillings and pence, to a Decimal system of dollars and cents. The Public Education Unit of the JIS collaborated with the Bank of Jamaica and produced a booklet called "Decimal Currency in Jamaica." JIS Radio and TV went to work to make sure that every radio listener and TV viewer became acquainted with the new money as quickly as possible. It was a very successful campaign, and was one of the two occasions I can remember when the Minister became personally involved with the work of the JIS. As the Minister in charge of finance he had to make absolutely sure that everything went alright. He also became personally involved with the Radio series "Life in Hopeful Village," written by Elaine Perkins. The series dealt with community development in which he had a keen interest.

When anyone outside, however influential, tried to interfere in the work of the JIS, he always stood by us. Once a high-ranking party member strode angrily into JBC and loudly demanded that we take a certain Australian–born caucasian woman off air. She was producing and hosting a music series for JIS. I immediately contacted the Minister, and he said he would deal with it. We heard no more from the angry gentleman, and, as far as I know, he never came near the JIS again.

Earlier in 1969, the British Central Office of Information (COI) invited Lloyd DePass, General Manager of Radio Jamaica. Barbara Gloudon, Features Editor of the Gleaner and I to do a tour of England. Lloyd Depass dropped out at the last moment. Barbara and I left on May 2. The tour was to last for about twenty days.

The publishing house, William Collins and Sangster (Jamaica) Ltd, had accepted my manuscript: "The Fighting Maroons of Jamaica." It would be published that year. I would meet their people in London to receive advance copies. That alone would make the trip worthwhile. Among other things, I roamed briefly through Westminister Abbey; which was full of tombs and monuments. I was delighted to pose for pictures in front of the huge, magnificent equestrian statue of Richard Lion-heart, the only thing that came close to Bismarck's awe-inspiring monument at Hamburg in Germany.

In Nottingham (by a wall that was all that was left of Nottingham Castle) I amused myself by posing beside the statue of Robin Hood. The most curious moment for me was when I was invited to an old rectory to have tea with a very elegant and correct lady. She chided me mildly for turning up dressed in jacket and tie rather than in my "national costume." I couldn't imagine where her "head was." The brightest moment of course was the day I received four copies of "The Fighting Maroons of Jamaica" from William Collins and Sangster.

Anyone who has ever had a book published for the first time will understand the mysterious emotion of joy and wonder at seeing one's work in print. I was awestruck and happy.

What impressed me the most, however, was the free-moving presence of Jamaicans in England; notwithstanding the "natural" problems of discrimination in an insular and conservative host-society. So different from the Jim Crow menace of my student days in the US. On my way back to the hotel in London one day, I ran into a policeman from the mounted troop in Jamaica, who had taken part in the film "Time of Fury." He recognized me at once and we had a nice chat. He was attending a course at a riding school and seemed relaxed and confident. At the castle Tobacco Factory of John Player and Sons Ltd in Nottingham, we saw Jamaican girls working cheerfully beside their British counterparts. The atmosphere was friendly. Black girls from humble backgrounds quickly found that, unlike in Jamaica, white girls did the same kind of work that they did, in factories and elsewhere. We saw Howard Hendricks, an apprentice from Jamaica, at work at the Ruston-Bucyrus Ltd. in Lincoln. They manufacture earth moving and agricultural machinery. A confident-looking young man. The Central Office of Information (COI) kindly let me have a television set in my hotel room. I was impressed with the programming. The public-affairs programmes were frank and hard-hitting. Comedy shows made fun of the racial situation and took a lot of sting out of it and made racial pre-occupation seem childish. Black people were in everything: TV shows, singing groups, scouts and guide troops, rugby and football teams. Wherever they did well, they were applauded. It was heart-warming to see the beaming faces of the young. Years later I heard talk of racial slurs aimed at the Jamaican football professionals in places like Liverpool; but I can only speak here of what I saw and felt. Jamaicans and other West Indians were accepted into industrial training institutions, like everyone else, and were learning all sorts of valuable skills. The older ones from the deep, rural areas didn't appear to have changed much. They still looked, spoke and acted like Jamaican country people. We met a group of them and Barbara Gloudon had a great time rapping with them in Jamaica creole. They responded warmly. The younger ones however, were already a different breed. To put it crudely they were "Black English." Better still: they were second generation English people. Whatever their problems, they were definitely not cowed.

I was glad to be away from my desk for the three week visit, but I was also happy to board the plane for home, on Thursday, May 22.

When we stopped at New York a strange thing happened. We had to wait awhile for the flight to Jamaica. I got tired of sitting in the waiting area and took a walk around, looking at the in-bond shops and other things. I could clearly hear the announcements for the departure of various flights, so I wasn't worried. I sat down and relaxed awhile, then thought I had better go back to the waiting area. When I got there the area was empty. My hand luggage containing my passport, etc. was not where I had left it. I hurried to an attendant and was told that the passengers had already boarded and the plane was getting ready to take off. I ran like a madman down the corridors and stairways to the entrance door of the tarmac. The plane was just beginning to taxi to the runway. *"I'm supposed to be on that plane,"* I said breathlessly. But the airport personnel barred the way. *"You can't go out there now,"* they said, *"it's too late."* I cannot describe the feeling of incredulity and horror which gripped me. My wife would be waiting for me at the Palisadoes (Norman Manley) Airport. The airlines people sent a message up to Kingston about my predicament, and agreed to put me up at an airport hotel for the night. I had no documents, no luggage and only a little money in my wallet. I bought a disposable razor, and spent the night in the hotel room, watching horror movies on the TV (Frankenstein and the rest).

I was up early the next morning, determined to be at the airport well ahead of time. I was probably the first person to report at the airlines desk. They knew all about me, and I had no trouble. This time I sat down and just waited. I was taking no more chances; for I just couldn't understand how I missed the boarding call the day before.

When the call came for passengers to board for Jamaica I was very near the head of the line. I boarded without any travel documents and landed the same way; glad to get home after that hair-raising experience.

It turned out that Barbara Gloudon, not seeing me appear when the boarding call came, had taken up my hand luggage with the travel document. She didn't think it would have been safe to just leave it there in the empty waiting area.

The Hatchet Man Appears

1970 started off quite well. I went to Guyana for a Broadcasting Information Conference, from March 24 – 27. All the bright Caribbean broadcasters were there, most of them Information types like myself. They seemed as good as any group of young people I had come across anywhere. And yet, there was a shadow of uncertainty as to what we stood for, and where we were heading.

I found Guyana to be vastly unlike Jamaica. Most of the life of the country seemed crowded on a strip of land running along a two hundred and seventy miles shore line. Behind that the country stretched six hundred miles; bordered by Venezuela, Brazil and Suriname. And on the far south and west, the plains ran into Mount Roriama, which rises over nine thousand feet, on the border with Brazil and Venezuela. We didn't get into the plains or mountains. We hung around the sea-coast strip, in the area where the capital Georgetown stands. I liked the fairly un-hurried small-town atmosphere, and enjoyed an evening's entertainment in the home of one of the Guianese delegates. It was informal and friendly; unpretentious. You didn't feel hit on the head by any consciously lavish life-style meant to impress.

Guyana became independent in 1966, four years after Jamaica. I remember a Guyanese journalist named Claude Robinson telling me that Guyana encouraged miscegenation, which is probably a positive move in a multi-racial society that aims at racial equality. But in the early 1960s there was a lot of racial tension and violence, accompanied by a long period of strikes. A new proportional representational system gave Forbes Burnham the opportunity to oust the leftist party, headed by East Indian Cheddi Jagan. When Burnham led the country into independence at the head of a coalition Government, there was still a lot of racial tension, primarily between East Indians and people of African descent.

In Guyana I met people like Hugh Cholomondeley. Hugh was an excellent broadcaster, but he was one of those who would feel the heavy metal fist of intolerant politics, which would knock him away from the country. But in those conference days, we were all full of proud West Indian hopes. We were the new people of the world.

In April 1970, not long after I returned to Jamaica, I was one of seven persons honoured with Musgrave medals by the Institute of Jamaica. I got a silver for "a high standard of Broadcasting." At around this time, trouble began to build up again at JBC. After a desperate search, a new manager was hired. Shortly after, it was thought wise to send him off on a management training course.

There was something surreal and unrealistic in the belief that anyone could be trained to run a Jamaican national broadcasting institution through a sit-in, walk-through and look-see exercise. It was the most prestigious, well-funded, well-staffed and well-equipped metropolitan broadcasting institutions which did not suffer from awesome deficiencies and limitations which faced the JBC. We had apparently learnt nothing since 1959, when Peter Aylen was brought in to set up and run JBC. The new manager was duly sent off to a course at the BBC, and for attachments at the Canadian Broadcasting Corporation (CBC),and the National Broadcasting Company of New York (NBC). NBC was the big daddy, the big brother, the indispensible adviser of the independent JBC. Shortly after the departure of the new man, big daddy (NBC) was asked to send down an expert to reorganize and restructure the JBC. He reported directly to the Board. Laurie Stewart, the Chief Engineer was made acting general manager. The NBC expert told him bluntly not to interfere in anything he was doing. The expert took off his expert's mask and revealed the countenance of a hatchet man. He went through the place like a conqueror, subduing staff and flexing his muscles. If he had been an exceptional kind of person (in a positive sense) things might have come off better. But he had the arrogant spirit of a conqueror and subduer.

As he roamed about, thinking of ways to re-organize and restructure, he sometimes came across to the studio when JIS was rehearsing or transmitting. He watched our programmes and listened to comments on our work. He soon got the brilliant idea that to strengthen JBC's Programmes Department, the Corporation should take over JIS-TV. When I heard the suggestion I was outraged. I was furious. I made it clear that such a proposal was out of order, and out of the question. I figured no one in his senses would try to take this man seriously. In the meantime we were very much aware of the disaffection of some senior JBC staff, and of attempts by others to gain an advantage by "sucking up" to the Hatchet man. He made it plain to the engineers that resignations coming from them wouldn't bother him, for there were people who could be recruited from abroad to take their jobs. Well, the thing about the world is that it is quite prepared to accept the values we place on ourselves. Show the world an attitude of dependence, and very soon you'll get a hatchet man who will be happy to oblige, and take over. The General Manager was away for about two and a half months, and was told in the meantime not to interfere as the Corporation was being reorganized. By the time he returned he had been sidelined, and the Hatchet was in charge. Painful attempts were made to recover his position, but it was too late. The situation was untenable. His days were numbered. As a board member, I read correspondence from the Hatchet to the GM. I was appalled at the contemptuous, insulting and bullying language. I had to go to the GM's office and tell him how sorry I was about the whole thing. I didn't think any Jamaican should be subjected to this sort of treatment from any foreign expert.

I had my own encounter with the Hatchet man; a very brief one, at the highest level of the civil service. The Permanent Secretary in our ministry phoned and invited me to a meeting in his office with the Hatchet and a senior JBC member, to discuss matters to do with JBC and JIS. I told the Permanent Secretary quite politely that if it had anything to do with a proposal to place JIS-TV under the Corporation's umbrella, I would ask to be excused. He assured me that no such matter would be discussed. Shortly after the meeting started, however, the matter was raised. Completely surprised at what appeared to be a deception, I turned to the Permanent Secretary and reminded him that he had assured me the subject would not be discussed. He blundered around a bit and said something about just wanting to explore the possibilities. I jumped up and said I would not discuss the subject. So I had better leave. He started to remonstrate but I stormed out of the office, not sparing a thought for the fact that I was walking out on my Permanent Secretary, in front of others.

Sometime later, when I had cooled down a bit, I figured that the Minister had been approached, perhaps by the chairman, and the matter had been referred to the Permanent Secretary. The poor man would have had no real alternative but to try and bring about a discussion. I never knew what was happening in the background; what strings were being pulled and what agendas were being set. I tried never to operate in that manner myself, and I was sick and tired of deceit. I received no reprimand for my actions, but I was most surprised when, after the poor general manager resigned, I was again approached to take the job. I thought I had already killed and buried that possibility for good. Once again I said I didn't want the job. However, I was beginning to feel that the Almighty must have some plan for me, that could only be realized through JBC, I was being worn down. I felt weary and uncertain; helpless and a little afraid. In this frame of mind I attended a luncheon at the Terra Nova Hotel one day. We had just sat down, and lunch was being served, when someone hurried up and whispered in my ear that the Prime Minister wanted to speak to me urgently on the telephone. I excused myself and went to the telephone. The Prime Minister said he wanted to see me right away.

I got in my car and drove over to see him, full of apprehension. When I was ushered into his presence I was surprised to see Ivan Levy there. Ivan was sitting, but Prime Minister Shearer was on his feet. Without going into preliminaries he informed me that he was personally requesting me to take the job. He wanted to know what I was afraid of. I lied, and told him I wasn't afraid of anything. Well, it was done now. Without delay I packed all my stuff at JIS and took it home. I dared not look back. Someone once told me that if you had to go swimming in ice-cold water, the best thing was to dive in quickly. I said goodbye to no one. The JIS-TV staff particularly appeared to be outraged. I had worked very closely with them, on an almost daily basis, for about eight years.

Not long after, while I was at a cocktail party at Jamaica House, the Attorney General, Victor Grant, came up to me and said:-

"Do you know what are the three most difficult jobs in Jamaica?"

"No," I replied.

and he said:-

"Prime Minister, Attorney General and General Manager of JBC."

I went over to JBC as general manager on secondment from my substantive post as head of JIS. From the letter I had written to the Minister, Ivan Levy was well aware of how I felt about the post of general manager. He was at pains to assure me that, within reason, I would be given a free hand to carry out my duties, subject to the Corporation's policies. He asked me what I wanted to do about the Hatchet man. Did I wish to keep him on to assist me? I told him I didn't want any help of that kind. He requested me to speak to him, and I agreed. Perhaps there was some fear of offending NBC, who, after all, had helped to set up JBC, and were the Corporation's consultants. It seemed wise to maintain the goodwill of such a powerful organization.

I understood all that. I understood that we were a small and not very-well off country, too recently freed from subjections to be able to trust each other's capacities, and perhaps with good reasons. We could not afford to be carelessly offensive. But I felt that the whole business of nationhood was ridiculous if we had to sacrifice self-esteem. And, as with the nation, so with the individual. Literature is full of the scant regard paid to people like us, and often we invite it. The only way to develop spiritual muscle is to attempt what is difficult, instead of always going around "Cap in Hand."

I made an appointment with the Hatchet and he invited me for lunch at his apartment. I believed he prepared the lunch himself. It was good. He talked about recent events in a relaxed and friendly manner, and sort of explained why he had to be so tough. Strangely, I began to feel sorry for him. It was possible his superiors in New York might regard his mission as unsuccessful, if the assignment was terminated. But at the moment, there was no way on earth I could function under the same roof with him, after his insensitive performance. I thanked him for the excellent lunch, but the assignment had to be terminated.

Ivan Levy asked me to accompany him and another board member for a visit to the top executives in New York. I had long passed the stage of being impressed by "Big-Daddyism" (if there is such a word), but I believed in courtesy. Ivan and his colleague had to return to Jamaica after a couple of days, but he insisted I go up to Canada to touch base with CBC big wigs. I went and met a few people; looked around and attended a symphony concert, which I enjoyed. Then it was back home, to serious business.

I got a flood of letters, cards and telegrams congratulating me on my appointment as General Manager. Many of them were from people I didn't really know, and I felt embarrassed by the unexpected outpouring of apparent goodwill. A well-known actor and broadcaster Reggie Carter, came into my office with a serious face, shook my hand and offered his condolences. I believe that he, at least, was sincere.

In The Belly Of The Whale

When I think now of what happened in those days, I can hardly believe it. Stranger than fiction. I had been associated with JBC from the beginning, going almost daily to the studios; and later to board meetings once a month. I was definitely no stranger. Yet, when I took up the post as GM, I felt as naked as the day I was born.

I started on April 1, 1971 "All fools Day." I thought it was somehow appropriate. I knew the Corporation was in deep trouble, but I did not realize it was on the verge of collapse. I had hardly sat down at my desk when I was told that the radio announcer on the early show had completed his shift and no one had turned up to relieve him. The Programme Manager for Radio had resigned some time before, and a producer/director/presenter was acting in the post. She had gone off somewhere, and as it turned out, was away for a few days. Nobody was in charge. The operator in the studio was playing records, as the early morning announcer had gone. I was shocked. I phoned JIS and asked a member of staff who had radio experience to come over and do the shift. The JIS officer was there in no time, took over the shift and did a good job. When the acting programme manager finally turned up, she was feeling no pain. Shortly after, she resigned. There was nobody in Radio willing or able to take her place, so a TV producer/director, Desmond Elliot with some radio experience, was temporarily put in charge. Radio was in bad shape. One announcer on the early morning shift had developed the habit of having beer for breakfast in the studio. One of his favourite tunes which he often played was:- "In heaven there is no beer, that's why I drink it here." He started to make irresponsible statements with a double meaning, which became increasingly vulgar in a sexual sense. On the morning when the matter was brought to my attention, he had reached a daring level of obscenity.

Kay Dupee, the Corporation's secretary, hurried into my office and asked if I had heard "The latest one." She told me what had been said, and I pulled him off the air.

The Television Department was in no better shape. The programme director had resigned and was about to migrate to Canada. He had been much abused by the Hatchet and could hardly wait to get out of the place. The financial controller and chief accounant had resigned in February. He had clashed with the Hatchet over unauthorized expenditure. Part of his responsibility was to see that the expenses did not get out of hand. But he found himself in a position where the only time he knew about unbudgeted expenditure was when the bills were presented for payment. The second in command was now acting in the post, with the help of an expensive financial consultant. Engineering was now called "Engineering and Building Services". It was a mistake to put the two things together. Building Services was responsible for keeping the Corporation clean and maintaining the buildings. The recently-hired director of engineering just didn't have the time for that. Consequently, the Corporation was dirty and its housekeeping facilities badly maintained.

The director of engineering was struggling without equipment. Shortly after his appointment, the Hatchet asked him to install certain facilities. He made a note to put them in his capital budget, since there was no money for them. Just before the Hachet left to go home for Christmas he asked about the request he had made. When the director told him what he had done, the Hatchet ordered him to go ahead, as he had full authority from the Board. But the GM and the financial team said "no", not until the budget was approved. The confused director, caught in the middle, took the "unprecedented step" of writing the Chairman for clarification.

All but three members of the Engineering staff went on sick leave as a mark of protest. They wrote the chairman saying they were concerned that the Hatchet had usurped the roles of GM, acting GM and department heads by giving orders directly to staff. Since that incident, the engineers had managed to throw off "the Malaise' as they called it, but their department remained badly in need of equipment.

The Public Relations Section was largely non-functional, and was primarily concerned with the annual fundraising programme "Nuggets for the Needy." Its promotional work had been transferred to the Sales Department. Sales, with "Tino Barovier", Tony Holman and Aston "Tommy" Thomas was intact and functioning; but appeared demoralized by the RJR competition.

News and Public Affairs had been lumped together under a director of news and public affairs. Conflict soon emerged. News, with its highly specialized skills and daily unremitting demands, had to have its own autonomy. Archie Lindo, veteran broadcaster from the early RJR days, was chief editor on the radio news desk. The chief editor for the TV news desk was Raymond Lewis, who had been with the Gleaner for many years. In charge of both desks was Consie Walters, another Gleaner veteran. Over all these senior newsmen was a director of news who reported to the director of news and public affairs. The director of news and public affairs was not a professional newsperson, and being chiefly occupied with producing programmes "in the public interest," often appeared to be marching to a different drumbeat. If anything went wrong it was difficult to pin down responsibility. Too many cooks in the kitchen. The director of news (another ex-Gleaner man) wanted to leave, and, when I arrived, I was requested to transfer him to another department. The unfortunate director of news was transferred to the leader-less TV Programmes Department. He went as a manager, not a director. He knew next to nothing about TV. Veterans in the TV Department resented his presence.

The disorganized condition of TV was brought home early one evening, when I was watching a live musical show. As the time drew near for the show to end, it became obvious that the director of the show was paying no attention to the clock. If he kept on, everything, including the news, would be pushed into a late start. I sent him a message to begin closing-off. The show kept going until it had run several minutes into the time of the next programme. I asked him to come to my office when he was finished. When he came over I asked him why he hadn't closed off his programme on time. He stared at me blankly. I tried to show him that what he had done had thrown out the entire evening's schedule. There was an uncomprehending look on his face, as if he didn't understand why he couldn't be allowed to do as he pleased.

In the midst of the general malaise there were loyal staff members who worked with dedication: telephone operators, receptionists; secretaries, sales and traffic personnel, people in news who simply wanted to do a professional job, studio cameramen and technicians, the producers of the popular radio show "Teenage Dance Party," the producers of "The Lou and Ranny Show" and the engineers who carefully nursed worn-out equipment. They were proud of having designed and built a television mobile unit to cover the Commonwealth Games back in 1966.

For years the mobile unit was the only regular operating TV mobile in the Commonwealth Caribbean. It opened the way for many important events to be brought live to television viewers, including the state funerals of a national hero and a Prime Minister, the Opening of Parliament, budget debates and the annual national festival.

Up to the time I took over as GM, almost six hundred outside broadcasts had been carried. There was the indomitable Kay Dupee, the Corporation's Secretary, who remained resolutely competent and faithful through thick and thin. Office helpers like Melita Morrison (with a welcome cup of warm tea), Rudolph Grey, the gardener, Asquith "Sarge" Reddie, driver, ex-soldier; young Gladstone Wilson, who had a definite flair for radio production and young Tony Patel, JBC's "Man in the Sky" giving traffic advice from an aeroplane.

It is not good to call names, some worthy ones always get left out. But names pop into my mind: such as Fay Mathews, Jean Woodstock, Daisy Colquhoun, Dorrit Levy, Winston Carby, Tony Holman and Tommy Thomas in sales; Rupert Linton, "Lindy" Delapenha, standing 4-square in sports and top engineers Rupert Bent and Newton James. But perhaps it was Asquith "Sarge" Reddie who epitomized what lay in the best of the JBC staff, at the time. He was a man who never abandoned his military posture and demeanor. Usually he was stern-faced, his eyes alert under heavy eyebrows. Respectful, but never putting himself out to win your favour.

Sarge was a tower of strength to the Radio staff and the News department, which were the two areas in particular where his job took him. When he was on duty he saw to it that his co-workers arrived on time. He had a built in understanding of the value of punctuality. If there was an emergency, Sarge would present himself without waiting to be asked. He helped news editors to collect copy, and he could operate camera or sound equipment if the need arose. When the short-lived Wareika Hills Receiving Station was being set up, Sarge was there, day and night, helping with the construction.

When Emperor Haile Selassie came in 1966 and there was that "rush" of the Rastafarians at the airport; Sarge stood his ground, and assisted reporters and cameramen in their coverage. Just his stalwart presence alone was reassuring.

One big triumph for JBC was "School's Challenge Quiz". Laurie Stewart and his wife, Hope, were at a cocktail party at the home of Board Chairman, K.H. Ivan Levy. The subject of television programmes came up. Hope quite frankly said that while there was a lot of entertainment material, the station was contributing nothing to education. Ivan Levy asked if she had any suggestions. Hope thought they should try something like a University Challenge, which was then running in the U.K.

Ivan Levy felt it was a good idea, but said it might be more workable at the high school level. He endorsed the project, and Hope agreed to help.

She put together about two thousand questions on cards, and assembled a panel of people to produce more questions and act as judges. Cameraman Bernard Chin became the first producer of the series. Rev. Phillip Hart was the first moderator backed up by Erica Allen. The series started as an outside broadcast, in about 1970, using the mobile unit which went to competing schools. After a couple of seasons, Hope with a growing family of small children, had to give up overall responsibility. But School's Challenge carried on, and at this time of writing (2008), is very much alive. Dennis Hall (an Ex- RAF man) was moderator for many years. So in spite of all the deplorable things at JBC, there was this "saving" body of staff who did the best they could, often under very difficult circumstances.

Driven partly by the heedless demands of the Hatchet, the previous GM had presented a budget which showed a considerable expenditure over expected revenue. The Board indignantly rejected it, and one of the first instructions I received was to "cut out all the fat" and come back with something that would indicate a profit. But even as the Board gave the order for a cut-back in expenditure, they also expressed the desire for an increase in Jamaican programames.

In spite of the mandate to hold down expenditure, I felt I had to give the Corporation a much needed face-lift, however limited. The Board gave me permission to upgrade the shabby front yard. I hired equipment, pushed the car park to the fence line, asphalted the area and got in some new plants. It was a scene of chaos for a day or two, with the bulldozer and asphalt equipment roaring up and down. But when it was over the place was transformed. The gardener, Rudolph Grey went to work eagerly with the new plants. On June 13, we put out a really good supplement in the Sunday Gleaner, to mark the twelfth anniversary of JBC, which fell on the following day (Monday, June 14). I wrote a starry-eyed statement which said:

> We have a unique opportunity to serve Jamaica. Our job calls us to the front line, where the action is. We work in an arena of events, exposed to the public gaze. Our work cannot be hidden and our efforts are far reaching, affecting the lives of hundreds of thousands in a single day's hard endeavor. We are the amplified voice of our country and a huge reflector of its culture. If one is off-key, we can do incalculable harm.

> We serve at a time when our country stands on the edge of discovery. The weight of creative interpretation and authentic expression of our national psyche falls in great measure on our shoulders. So it is necessary to be skillful, confident, intelligent, considerate, dedicated,

adventurous and relentless in the pursuit of our goals.

On the springboard of our twelfth anniversary, we rid our selves of things that hamper... and leap.

Leap indeed! In a comparatively short time I would be taking a terrific leap myself.

General Elections

When I was head of JIS I was invited to numerous cocktail parties, receptions, lunches, dinners and occasions of all sorts. Sometimes I had to make speeches and give out trophies. It went with the job, for JIS had earned a very good reputation. Now, JBC was more of the same, because JBC was still regarded as a very important high-profile national institution. The newspapers gave a lot of coverage, with photographs: much more than today, when radio stations are "a dime a dozen" and the prestigious power of Jamaican TV has been overtaken and almost submerged by the satellite dish and cable.

At the end of the rather hectic Calendar year, Chairman Ivan Levy expressed satisfaction with my handling of the Corporation. It is buried somewhere in the minutes books of the JBC, if they still survive. After about eight years as a board member, it was strange to be subjected to the scrutiny of my former board colleagues. I felt somewhat "demoted."

My salary was nothing to shout about, although it was appreciably better than what I had earned at JIS. The Jamaican currency was strong. With two Jamaican dollars you could buy one British Pound. But back then I could live, and save something.

The shadow of the upcoming General Elections now began to loom large. Preoccupied as I was with the stressful conditions accompanying my transition from JIS to JBC, I hadn't thought much (if anything) about the elections. But now the approaching event began to stare me in the face. Political activity increased in one or two places within the Corporation. It had to be handled carefully to avoid walking into traps. Soon the time arrived for the political parties to make their election broadcasts, which had to be done in accordance with rules and regulations laid down in the licenses of both stations (JBC and RJR).

An awkward situation arose when the Leader of the Opposition and Head of the PNP, Michael Manley, came to the station with his entourage and his "rod of correction," to record his speech. The rod of correction was a big stick which Mr. Manley carried during his election campaign. The senior officer in charge of overseeing the recording of political broadcasts conveniently disappeared sometime during the proceedings. I was sitting in my office when a junior officer phoned to say that Mr. Manley's speech had gone beyond the time limit, and that the rod had been use to dramatize certain statements. The regulations strictly forbade the use of dramatizations during political broadcasts. The junior officer requested that I come to the studio and decide what should be done. I went over and told Mr. Manley I was sorry, but he would have to shorten his speech and not use the rod. In effect that meant he would have to record it again. "But I am hoarse" he said; and indeed he did sound hoarse. I said I was sorry, but I had to go by the rules. He was unhappy but he got to work with his team, right there in the studio, cut the speech, and recorded it again, without the use of the rod.

The failure of the senior officer to see to the proper recording of the important speech was the sort of thing that undermined the reputation and effectiveness of the JBC. The officer had deliberately ducked out of the responsibility. But there was more to come. The Government requested live coverage of the announcement of the date of the General Elections. The announcement was to be made at a public meeting either preceding a speech, or right after the speech; I forgot which. Instructions were given that only the section concerning the announcement of the date was to be carried live. But the whole speech was carried live, and it was a vigorous electioneering speech. The opposition PNP was furious, and demanded equal time to compensate for this unauthorized "political broadcast." The senior officer, who had allowed it all to happen, again slipped quietly into the shadows.

The Opposition demanded to see me at once. I had a quick discussion with the chairman and then met their top-level delegation. After listening to their heated arguments, which could not be honestly refused, I made up my mind to give them extra time. That same day, I received a letter from Michael Manley dated February 1. It was signed on his behalf by someone whose signature I couldn't make out. It was a diplomatic letter, a model of understatement. But beneath the restrained words I detected a dire threat. Mr. Manley's letter said:-

> *I wish to refer to the speech of the Honorable Hugh Shearer, Leader of the Jamaica Labour Party, on Monday 31st January, 1972, when he presented the candidate for Central Kingston and announced the date of the general elections. It has not escaped my notice that his speech was carried live and virtually in its entirety. In fact, the telecast lasted in excess of twenty minutes. During this time he was permitted to state the platform of his party, to make accusations against the Opposition and only the actual announcement of nomination day and election day itself could possibly be regarded as being of legitimate national importance. I would remind you of your letter to me of 18th January 1972, in which you "consolidated a number of rules" that were designed to prevent undue advantage on any side. It is most important*

that as a public corporation you preserve an at-mosphere of total impartiality during this cam-paign. Whatever treatment is afforded one side I expect to be afforded to the other.

I am writing to request that your station indicate its preparedness to afford me the same time and courtesy extended to the Labour Party on both radio and television for me to speak to the nation.

As soon as your confirmation is forthcoming we can discuss the time and manner of its implementation.

Fortunately I agreed with the position Mr. Manley had taken, so there was no need to agonize over a decision. Only a direct order from the Chairman could change things, and that would surely have resulted in my resignation. But I didn't expect that from Ivan Levy.

A team from the Opposition got some film footage and put a broadcast together. The PM was not amused. Ivan Levy looked sad and tired, like a besieged soldier who had fired his last bullet. But there was nothing else to be done, without violating the integrity of the Corporation.

For me it was a "no-win" situation. Heads you win, tails you lose. I ended up with both sides having cause to be unhappy with me. There were dark rumours that my "head was going to roll".

The General Elections were set for February 29, 1972. The Parliament was dissolved on February 5. Certain individuals on the staff got hysterical, and demanded that additional security be put in place at the Corporation on election night. They feared an assault on JBC by militant members in the public, if the results went contrary to their wishes. They wanted soldiers brought in. I don't recall that the Board granted that request. Ivan Levy and several members of the Board gathered in the board room during the early hours of the broadcast of election results. The atmosphere was uneasy. Ivan smoked, perhaps more than usual. All watched tensely as the results rolled in, peeping now and then through the window which overlooked the busy studio scene. As night fell the results didn't look good for the government.

Suddenly, after one particularly devastating result, Ivan Levy jumped up and said: *"Well, that's that. I'm going home. I'll be sending in my resignation from the Board tomorrow."* He had no illusions about his position. Others in the room stirred sluggishly. I tried to persuade Ivan to hang on a little longer. I knew he was right, but I was mentally holding back from the brink of imminent change. I had only been at the Corporation for about ten months and the dust of previous events had just begun to settle. This looming crisis was coming too soon. But Ivan Levy brushed aside my protestations. The hand writing was on the wall. There was no point pretending. He said goodnight to everyone and left abruptly. After awhile the rest shuffled out. I believe I was left alone (or almost alone) in the board room.

When it was obvious that the governing party had lost the elections, a group of militants who had been hovering outside the gates, stormed into the compound with shouts of victory; ran into the Television building and down the passageway and broke into the studio, yelling that "their time had come".

People can say whatever they want to, about the cordial relations, the friendship and goodwill that existed between the top leaders of the opposing factions. But all I saw during that period was savage warfare, in which there was always the danger that the rules of war might be broken in the interest of victory. And while the top leaders might grin at each other in public, shake hands and slap each other on the back, the lower rank, on either side, were engaged in a deadly struggle. The seriousness of this growing "tribal" conflict had surfaced during the JBC strike. But now it was becoming ever more lethal, and JBC was a focal point, a mirror of that struggle. It had become one of the coveted spoils of war. It was the only TV station, the only means at that time to gain access to the enormous and ever-expanding world of TV. It seemed that whoever controlled the magic box of TV, would be in a strong position to manipulate the national mind. Every Jamaican who could afford it (or could ill-afford it) was buying a TV, and gathering in front of it with the family every evening to soak up everything. But JBC had no real power to save a government when its time came to fall. It was unreasonable to endow it with such power.

The preliminary count of votes on March 1, 1972, gave victory to the PNP. Michael Manley was sworn in as Prime Minister on March 2. It is said that after being sworn in by the Governor General, the first place he visited was JBC. It was evident that the Corporation had become an important symbol. Together with the university, it contained an aroused section of the young "middle class" which seemed to be waiting for something. When the new PM entered the JBC compound there was a rush from all sides to see him. Even the JIS staff in the old Educational Broadcasting Services building at 5 South Odeon, ran to the windows to see him. I went out into the yard and shook his hand and someone took a picture of it. He must have remembered that broadcast I made him do over. He had a smile for everyone. There was a holiday mood. Later, in my office, over a glass of white wine, he told Laurie Stewart and myself that he wanted us "to stay on." After a brief period of waiting a new Board was appointed. The new chairman was a seasoned one-time trade unionist, a popular journalist and commentator, and a former left-wing politician. A different personality from Ivan Levy could hardly be imagined. Prime Minister Manley made an official visit to the Corporation shortly after. He went through every section and met all the

Prime Minister Michael Manley's visits to the Corporation.

members of staff who were present. I think this intimate tour by a head of Government was unprecedented; certainly not since the days of Norman Manley (the PM's father) when JBC was set up; and then it had been a very different place. After his tour, the Prime Minister addressed the new Board in the boardroom. He told them with a serious face what he expected of them. But I can't remember the details of what he said.

The new chairman's style tended to be confrontational, in the manner of one who had been accustomed to worker/management relationships that were hostile and distrustful. His first directive was to invite all members of staff who had a grievance to bring it to the Board. It was an open door to all malcontents and mischief-makers. It certainly couldn't have been intended to foster good worker/ management relations, or to strengthen the role of management.

There was a "business faction" on the Board which wasn't so much concerned with workers/ management relations as with making the Corporation a profitable business. They were ignorant of how the commercial media in the U.S. functioned, and did not understand, or chose to ignore, what JBC was initially set up to do. One of them thought that TV was "a licence to coin money." They seemed to think that what we were trying to do was the equivalent of selling cloth, or making garments for export. The new chairman was not well. In a short time he appeared quite shaky. Board members stirred restlessly. It seemed that soon, another change was likely to take place. In the meantime, the threat of a wedge being driven between management and staff hung over us. My mind went back to my student days, when Norman Manley had come to Howard, and given us a vision of being free and independent; taking charge of the high and difficult tasks; building a nation and being responsible for its future. Now, ten years after we got independence, we were divided into hostile camps, discriminating against each other, tearing at one another; suspicious, distrusting. The day after the PNP victory a relative of mine phoned me in high glee and said: *"What happen, Labourite; them gone with you now!"* It shocked me. As far as my relative was concerned politics had been the determining factor in my career. It took me back to the JLP win in 1962, when a senior member of the old Government Public Relations Office had suggested I joined him in resigning, rather than work for a new government. The "fault" in our national façade had cracked open at the moment of Independence.

In June, 1972, a little over two months after he had been sworn in as Prime Minister, Michael Manley married Beverly Anderson, a radio and television personality known for her sleepy-eyed look on TV. I was at home having breakfast when the phone rang. Basil McFarlane was on the line, an old school-mate of mine from Calabar days. We used to call him "Bad Bill", after a cowboy novel of the same name which he prized highly. He was the eldest son of J.E. Clare McFarlane, the country's first Jamaican Financial Secretary and Poet Laureate. Bad Bill, who was a poet himself, was very close to the Manleys. He told me that Michael wanted to see me now. His tone irritated me. The Prime Minister was at his mother's place in the Drumblair Housing Scheme. I said I was having breakfast but would leave as soon as I was finished. Norman Manley had long sold his old Drumblair home, and the land had been subdivided for housing lots. He reserved one for himself and built a modest home on it which he called "Regardless". I always thought the name was a cry of defiance.

When I drove up to Regardless, Mrs. Edna Manley, Norman Manley's widow, was speaking to someone in the front yard. As I walked towards the house she said: "Just a minute" and stopped me. "Who are you?" she asked. I told her, and said I had been asked to come. Quite unexpectedly she asked, "When were you born?" I told her. She then said "Oh, you're under the same sign as Michael. You can go in."

I walked through the house. The PM was no-where in sight, but his brother, Douglas Manley was sitting on the back porch speaking to some people. Douglas told me that Michael and Beverly had been married that morning, and we discussed the contents of the news items to be used on JBC.

In September, the Tourist Board invited me to participate in a promotional tour to Atlanta, Georgia. Shortly after my return from Atlanta, the question of our representation at the Ninth Commonwealth Broadcasting Conference came up. It was to be held in Kenya. I had tried to duck out of the Seventh conference in Nigeria; but, looking back, I was glad I went.

But now, as GM of JBC, it was imperative that I represent the Corporation at the Kenya Conference. I didn't want to leave my desk so soon again. The conference was scheduled to run October 16 to 27. Add another two or three days of travelling time. When I expressed reluctance to go everybody thought I was mad. I was just about commanded to go. Thank God. I would probably never get another chance to go to Kenya. And deep down I knew that my going or not going would have no effect on what was developing at the Corporation. Rupert Bent, the Director of Engineering, went with me.

Kenya

The unforgettable thing about the Kenya conference was Jomo Kenyatta himself. A short, stocky man who seemed like a giant. Years ago at RJR, during the Mau Mau uprising in Kenya, Fred Wilmot got himself "fired" for writing sympathetically about Jomo Kenyatta and Mau Mau. I remember seeing Jomo's picture in a magazine in some sort of African clothes, holding a spear. They had called him the "Burning Spear" then, and he seemed like the most dangerous man in the world. He had been tried and convicted of being the leader of the Mau Mau. I had thought he would be executed, but he was imprisoned for seven years, with an additional two years of confinement. He got his freedom when Kenya's two political parties insisted he be released. They considered him to be the leader of the country and he was elected as its first Prime Minister in 1963. He was made the first President in 1964, when Kenya became a republic on its first anniversary of its Independence.

He opened the Ninth Commonwealth Broadcasting Conference on the morning of Tuesday, October 16, 1972. I remember him standing on the platform when Kenya's National Anthem was being played. He lifted his ornate fly switch over his head, and his eyes, which were already large and haunting, seemed to grow more and more, to twice their natural size. They were hypnotic. People said he was a Master Wizard and he seemed like one on that day. He looked beyond everyone while the anthem was being played. He subdued the roomful of people and engulfed them. He seemed to grow, until the big room appeared too small to hold him. But when the anthem was over it was just Jomo once more in his brimless hat, which looked as if it was made to be worn at a carnival.

When the ceremony was over, it amazed and delighted me to see Jomo put the point of his walking stick on the ground and hop lightly off the high platform like a boy of twelve. He was about eighty-two at the time. Later he was brought around to meet the heads of delegations. Dudley Thompson of Jamaica had helped to defend him in the time of his trial, and he never forgot that. So he had a special word for me when we shook hands. I spoke of Mr. Thompson to him.

Observing His Excellency, the Hon. Mzee Jomo Kenyatta, President of the Republic of Kenya, I understood how he got out of the clutches of the British Colonial power, how he came to hold all Kenya together despite dangerous tribal rivalries, and how he overshadowed the land like a fatherly titan. It was because he expressed life so powerfully, from its greatest depths. He came up fresh, even when he was eighty-two. He was not tied by the bonds which bind ordinary men.

I felt greatly honoured to be chosen to deliver the vote of thanks to Jomo at the inauguration. I was chosen because Jamaica had been the venue of the previous Commonwealth Broadcasting Conference.

On Kenyatta Day (October 20, in honour of Jomo Kenyatta) there were no conference meetings. Instead we attended the celebrations in Uhuru Park. We were given wide-brimmed floppy hats and sat in the bright sunlight in a special section of the crowded stands. The place was packed with a vast crowd. Jomo Kenyatta was on the platform with his tall, young and very attractive wife. He had the "fly switch" which he waved overhead at appropriate moments. In the afternoon we went to the Presidential Garden Party at the State house and witnessed the exhilarating sight of burly, old Jomo dancing with a girl of about twelve, to a rousing piece of music. He was light and easy on his feet, moving to the rhythms, expertly.

On the weekend we visited Nairobi National Park where we sat in vehicles and watched such animals as zebra, lion, leopard, hyena, elephant, rhinoceros, hippopotamus, antelope, gazelle, jackal, etc. Fantastic. I was greatly interested in the very tall, lean Masai warriors with shields and long deadly looking spears, with which they hunt lions.

We were invited to sample the night life of Nairobi, which turned out to be rather funny. We were taken to what was said to be one of the city's famous night spots. Our host drove through various streets until we arrived at a strange looking building from which music came. The place looked drab. The architecture was disturbing; more like a market that was closed, than a night club. A garish light illuminated the entrance, and at the apex of the roof was a large blue outline of a star made of neon lights. The interior of the building was gloomy. In the semi-darkness a band was crashing out a tune. Thanks to our host we got in free. "This is the Starlight Club," he said. He was a Jamaican working on contract to the Government of Kenya. "The Starlight used to be a church," he added. So that was what accounted for the architectural strangeness. In the big high ceiling room, I did get the feeling of being in a derelict church. Our host took us through the dancing couples to a large square garden at the rear of the building. It had many tables and chairs and a couple of thatched-roof bars. We sat at a table. Three young women emerged from the gloom of the dancing hall and approached. One was very tall and big, with a high halo of hair. *"Is she a Masai?"* I asked our host. *"she's tall enough,"* he replied, *"but too big."* As they drew near, our host, who seemed to be a regular customer at the Starlight, sprang up, and invited them to sit. *"Are you a Masai?"* I asked the very tall one. *"I'm a Luo,"* she said. They all spoke fairly good English. After some vigorous dancing (I danced with the giant Luo) we had a rice-based meal, and returned to the hotel to prepare for the next day's conference activities.

A couple of days later, the priest I met at the conference in Nigeria, and who had introduced us to the Nigerian "High Life" music, volunteered to take us to a lively place in the city, so we could see Nairobi by night. We accepted. I was curious to see how the priest's choice would compare with the Starlight. I believe he had fled from Nigeria, because of the Civil War. Now he seems to be a part of the Kenyan delegation. When the car stopped and we go out, we were surprised to see that gloomy pile once more, with the blue neon star. The Starlight. Our bearded host had the air of a man who was about to introduce his honoured guests to a pleasant experience. Like proper gentlemen, we didn't have the heart to disillusion him. Again we got in free, although the cashier, who recognized us, looked skeptical.

The next day, the Conference Committee planned an outing for us which was to take place that night. We were to visit an interesting place which was a must for all visitors to Nairobi. We drove through unfamiliar streets, well away from the Starlight it seemed. That was a relief. When the car stopped and we got out, we were stunned. There before us was an ominous blue neon star on top of a gloomy structure. We walked towards that incongruous one-time church, like men in some Greek tragedy, who arrive at the same spot, regardless of what road they took. We were now convinced that Starlight was the very heart and centre of Nairobi night life. This time, we had to pay to get in. The place was full of conference delegates, who appeared to be there for the first time. We, of course, had the jaded look of veterans.

Outer Space

Back in Jamaica, the new chairman of the JBC became seriously ill and had to resign. Another unsettling period was ushered in. The in-coming chairman was again a very different type. Two or three changes were also made on the still-new Board. Influencing all the shuffling were tough and radical policies which the new government was instituting.

When I brought up the sensitive subject of "impartiality," a senior board member said: "Look Carey, I took six months leave from my job to work for the party." And that was that.

Hector Bernard returned to JBC from an assignment as information officer at the Jamaica Embassy Department, much to my relief. We sat in my office and listened to Michael Manley's first speech in Parliament as Prime Minister. Michael was in top form and seemed irresistible. I saw him at a function on the open-air roof top patio of the Gleaner Company. He was extremely well-dressed, in jacket and tie, and seemed to be glowing from an inner flame; more handsome than ever. Looking back now I am struck by the impermanence of the whole passing parade. Jeremy Verity, who had been with the BBC, was appointed to head the Corporation's long-suffering Radio Department. Jeremy was the half-brother of Rachel Manley, Michael Manley's first child. He was a large serious looking young man. Again it was a relief to have him in charge of radio.

A major event during my time at JBC was the Sunshine Showdown: the Heavyweight champion-ship fight between "Smoking" Joe Frazier and George Foreman in Jamaica.

A stern faced Archie Moore came with Frazier, as his trainer, I believe, Smoking Joe and Archie were standing apart from the milling, excited crowd at Jamaica House where a reception was being held by Prime Minister Michael Manley. Foreman appeared to be the centre of attention. I went up to Smoking Joe and Archie, greeted the serious-looking Frazier and reminded grim-faced Archie of the series he had done on JIS. His face relaxed grudgingly into the ghost of a smile. JBC produced the commercials for the event and broadcast the fight. It seemed to me that Frazier kept leading with his head, and Foreman was using it as a punching bag. The fight was soon over. Frazier went down like a spiraling fighter plane crashing uncontrollably to earth.

Roughly two and a half years after I took up the post of general manager I handed in my resignation. The last couple of months had been progressively uncomfortable. I was a hold-over from the old regime, and the politically-appointed Board was under-standably uncomfortable with me in their midst. Neither my father nor I had foreseen a time when a desire to serve the country would not be enough.

Barry Davis, an Englishman who had worked with RJR while I was there, and who had done some programmes at JBC, came to my office and said: *"it must be tough to reach the top of one's profession and have to step-down."* I said: *"But is it the top?"*

For the truth is I had felt freer, more productive and more in charge at JIS. But even JIS, which had been so useful to the country, was soon to under-go a change, however temporary. I felt battered and abandoned; but as it turned out, this was not altogether the case. The Chairman of JBC persuaded me to attend a farewell meeting with senior members of staff. I hated farewells and had abruptly ducked out of JIS to avoid one. This situation was worse for I was angry. At the beginning of the meeting, after I had thanked the senior members of staff for their support during my term as GM, I said I was not staying for the rest of the ceremony and immediately walked to the door.

The chairman sprang up and in an urgent voice requested me to wait. I turned and stood in the open doorway while he did his best to thank me. Then I walked out of the building as fast as I could and drove home without a word to anyone, except for my excellent secretary, Olga Leslie, and Hector Bernard's secretary, Karlene Longmore. I took a silent oath that I would never again enter JBC. I swore that if I ever had to go past the place, I would turn my face away, so as not to see it. In my mind I shook the dust of the Corporation off my shoes.

But fate was to play a wretched trick on me. Some fourteen years later, I found myself back in the place again, as a board member, and then briefly as GM.

On the day of my departure from the JBC I was almost stunned when a handful of women from the Corporation appeared at my home. Fay Matthews and (I believe) tall, slim Dorrit Levy were among them.

Someone made a speech of appreciation, and I was given two presents: a blue-grey sweater and a brief case. They turned out to be very useful. I still have them.

One of the last things I did before leaving Jamaica was to drive along the South Coast towards St. Thomas, to the salt ponds. There was a dirt road leading off the main, to a beach just behind the ponds. It was a long stretch of clean sand.

It lay before me that day in all its sea washed beauty, bounded on the land side by sea-grape trees. Not a soul in sight; just a cruising sea-bird or two. The sun was bright, the sea green-blue and sparkling. No sound, except the waves and wind.

I walked and walked, bare footed. Peace enveloped me. I went into the water and swam, and then rested on the sand. It was as if I was saying goodbye to a part of me that would be gone forever, along with the foolish innocence of youth.

I drove to the Norman Manley Airport to catch a plane to take me to the U.S.A. I was still a civil servant and was going to take up a new assignment in Washington D.C. A female member of the JIS staff drove out all the way to the airport to see me off. Just before I boarded the plane I was told there was a telephone call for me. A female member of the JBC staff was on the line to tell me goodbye. When the plane stopped at Montego Bay, Carmen Patterson, a new member of the Corporation's staff in the West, was there to wave goodbye to me, all women, I couldn't understand it. I felt most unworthy of their concern and attention. And so I went off, into Outer Space. My wife and 18 year old daughter would follow later. In the US my daughter would make a new life for herself and become the mother of five lovely daughters.

As the plane rose into the air I fervently hoped that I was not too late to start a new life, somewhere in Outer Space.

Glossary

Cat: An African-American slang word which means a male person.

Evon Blake: He was awarded the *Commander of the Order of Distinction* for *outstanding public service in journalism,* by the Jamaican government. Born in the highlands of Jamaica, Blake was widely travelled and was a professional journalist for over 40 years – as news magazine publisher, reporter, author and columnist. His publication, the coffee table book *Beautiful Jamaica*, first published in 1970, is currently in its eighth edition.

House of Parliament: The legislative branch of the government of Jamaica. It is composed of a Senate and a House of Representatives. The Senate (upper house) comprises of 21 senators, and the House of Representatives (lower house) is made up of 63 (previously 60) Members of Parliament, elected to five year terms. The Parliament meets in Gordon House, at 81 Duke Street in Kingston. It was built in 1960 and named in memory of national hero George William Gordon.

Jim Crow: The state and local laws that were enacted in the United States between 1876 and 1965. The laws mandated racial segregation in all public facilities in Southern states of the former Confederacy (eleven southern states of the

United States of America between 1861 and 1865) with a separate status for Black Americans. Some examples of Jim Crow laws are the segregation of public schools, public places, public transportation, restrooms and restaurants for whites and blacks.

Morant Bay Rebellion: The Morant Bay Rebellion began on October 11, 1865, when Paul Bogle led 200 to 300 black men and women into the town of Morant Bay. The rebellion and its aftermath were a major turning point in Jamaica's history, and also generated a significant political debate in Britain, of which Jamaica was a colony at the time. Today, the rebellion remains controversial and is often mentioned by specialists in black and colonial studies.

University of the West Indies: The University of the West Indies (UWI) is an autonomous regional institution supported by and serving 17 English-speaking countries and territories in the Caribbean. It consists of three physical campuses at Mona (Jamaica), St. Augustine (Trinidad & Tobago) and Cave Hill (Barbados), and the Open Campus. The university was founded in 1948 as the University College of the West Indies (UCWI) at Mona in Jamaica, in special relationship with the University of London based on the recommendations of the Asquith Commission. The Commission was established in 1943 and reviewed higher education in the then British Colonies. The university achieved independent university status in 1962.

PUBLISHER'S NOTES

Carey Robinson did not end up in outer space. He is very much here on earth, alive and well, and still contributing to the development of his country. Now at the Creative Production and Training Centre (CPTC), where he is imparting his knowledge in the visual arts as a television producer and director, his journey continues.